Annabel Karmel

Top 100 Baby Purées

Annabel Karmel
Top 100 Baby Purées

100 quick and easy meals for a healthy and happy baby

EBURY
PRESS

First published in Great Britain in 2005

5 7 9 10 8 6 4

Text © Annabel Karmel 2005
Photographs © Dave King 2005

First published by Ebury Press
Random House, 20 Vauxhall Bridge Road,
London SW1V 2SA

Random House Australia (Pty) Limited
20 Alfred Street, Milsons Point, Sydney,
New South Wales 2061, Australia

Random House New Zealand Limited
18 Poland Road, Glenfield, Auckland 10, New Zealand

Random House South Africa (Pty) Limited
Endulini, 5A Jubilee Road, Parktown 2193, South Africa

The Random House Group Limited Reg. No. 954009

www.randomhouse.co.uk

A CIP catalogue record for this book is available from the British Library.

Editor: Kate Parker
Design and art direction: Smith & Gilmour, London
Photographer: Dave King
Food stylist: Dagmar Vesely
Props stylist: Jo Harris

ISBN 0091 90499 4
ISBN 9780091904999 (from Jan 2007)

Papers used by Ebury Press are natural, recyclable products
made from wood grown in sustainable forests.
Printed in Italy by Graphicom

Contents

Introduction

Starting solids

Babies grow more rapidly in their first year than at any other time in their life, so how you feed your newborn will be one of the most important decisions you make for your new baby.

Don't be in a hurry to wean your baby on to solids. For the first six months or so, breast milk or formula provides all the nutrients your baby needs, and should remain the main source of nourishment. Indeed, guidelines issued by the UK Department of Health recommend breastfeeding exclusively for this period.

At around six months, however, your baby will reach a stage where she needs solid foods as well as milk in her diet. For example, the store of iron that she will have been born with will have been used up and so it will be important to include iron-rich foods in her diet (see page 7).

There is no 'right' age at which to introduce solids, though, as every baby is different. However, solids should not be introduced before seventeen weeks after your child is born. A young baby's digestive system is not sufficiently developed before this time and there is a greater risk of allergy developing. If you feel that your baby needs solids earlier than at six months, speak to your health visitor or GP.

Signs that your baby is ready:
- still hungry after a full milk feed
- demands feeds more frequently
- wakes at night for a feed having previously slept through

Your baby's nutritional needs

The nutritional needs of babies and toddlers are different from those of an adult – a low-fat, high-fibre diet is good for a full-grown person but not appropriate for babies or young children as they need more fat and concentrated sources of calories and nutrients to fuel their rapid growth. With this in mind, it is best not to give low-fat dairy products, such as milk and yoghurt, to young children, but choose instead the full-fat variety.

Neither should they be given too much fibre, as it tends to be bulky and can fill them up before they take in all the nutrients they need for proper growth and development. In addition, excess fibre can also flush out valuable minerals and cause other problems such as diarrhoea. Consequently, fibrous foods like dried fruits and pulses should be given in moderation, as should wholemeal bread and wholegrain cereals like Weetabix. Likewise, fruit purées, such as apple, pear and plum, shouldn't be given too frequently.

Babies should eat a wide variety of fruit and vegetables, however, to ensure they have plenty of vitamins and minerals in their diet. After the first few weeks of weaning, make sure that, as well as fruit and vegetable purées, you give foods that are relatively high in calories, such as mashed avocado, fruit mixed with Greek yoghurt or Vegetables with Cheese Sauce (see pages 30, 55 and 71).

Iron is very important for your baby's mental and physical development. A baby is born with a store of iron that lasts for about six months. After this it is important that your baby gets the iron she needs from her diet. Iron in foods of animal origin, like red meat or poultry, is much better absorbed than iron in foods of plant origin, like green vegetables or cereal. Vitamin C helps boost iron absorption, so give your baby vitamin C-rich fruits like berry or citrus fruits (but not before six months – see page 8), or vegetables like broccoli or sweet pepper.

Vitamin supplements

For most babies vitamin supplements are probably unnecessary, so long as they are eating fresh food in sufficient quantity and drinking formula milk until the age of one. However, the Department of Health recommends that if your baby is being breastfed (breast milk doesn't contain enough vitamin D) or is drinking less than 500ml (18fl oz) of infant formula a day, you should give your baby vitamin supplements from six months to two years of age. Ask your health visitor for advice.

The benefits of homemade baby food

The ingredients of most commercial baby foods have been heated to a very high temperature and then cooled, in order to sterilise them. This gives them a very long shelf life (usually two years) but destroys a lot of the flavour and some of the nutrients in the process. There is nothing better for your baby than making your own fresh baby food, and it is cheaper than buying the commercial variety. You will know exactly what the ingredients are, you can introduce a wide range of foods and your baby will get used to eating like the rest of the family so the transition to family meals will be easier. Preparing larger quantities than you need and freezing small portions in ice-cube trays or small pots can save you time and effort.

The importance of milk in a baby's diet

As stated above, breast or formula milk should provide all the nutrients your baby needs in the first six months. Ideally, you should try to breastfeed your baby until he is at least six months (twenty-six weeks) old. Indeed, it's best not to give your baby anything apart from breast milk during that period. Even after your baby starts eating other foods, it is still really important to make sure he gets enough milk. Between six months and one year, babies should still be receiving a minimum of 500–600ml (18–20fl oz) of breast or formula milk a day.

Breast milk is always preferable to formula because, in addition to meeting all of your baby's nutritional requirements, it contains antibodies that will help your baby fight illness and infection. In addition, breastfeeding for six months has been shown to delay the onset and reduce the severity of allergies in children from families with a history of asthma, hay fever, eczema and food allergy.

You should continue to give breast or formula milk to your baby as his main drink for the whole of the first year, as cow's milk does not contain enough iron or other nutrients for proper growth. However, from six months full-fat cow's milk can be used in cooking – for example, when making a cheese sauce for your baby – and can also be given with his breakfast cereal.

The best first foods for your baby

Very first foods should be easy to digest and unlikely to provoke an allergic reaction. I find that root vegetables like CARROTS, SWEET POTATO, PARSNIP and SWEDE tend go down best with very young babies due to their naturally sweet flavour and smooth texture once puréed.

APPLE and PEAR make good first fruit purées. BANANA and PAPAYA do not require cooking provided they are ripe, and can be puréed or mashed on their own, or together, with a little breast or formula milk. It's important that you choose fruits that are ripe and have a good flavour, so it's best to taste them first yourself before giving them to your baby.

Another good first food is BABY RICE. Mixed with water, breast or formula milk, it's easily digested and its milky taste makes for an easy transition to solids. Choose one that is sugar-free and enriched with vitamins and iron. Baby rice also combines well with both fruit and vegetable purées.

Foods to avoid

BERRY and CITRUS FRUITS, including fruit juice like orange and lemon juice, can trigger a reaction but rarely cause a true allergy. They can be given from six months.

FISH and SHELLFISH should not be given before six months due to the risk of food poisoning and potential allergy.

HONEY should not be given before one year. Very occasionally honey can contain a type of bacteria that can result in a potentially serious illness known as infant botulism. After a baby is a year old, the intestine matures and the bacteria can't grow, so giving honey at that stage is no problem.

NUTS and SEEDS, including peanuts, peanut butter and other nut spreads, should be strictly avoided if there is any risk of allergic reaction, such as a family history. Peanut butter and nut spreads can be given from six months provided there is no history of allergy in the family. Whole nuts of any kind are not recommended before the age of five due to the risk of choking.

RAW or LIGHTLY COOKED EGGS should be strictly avoided due to the risk of salmonella infection.

Eggs should not be given before six months and should be cooked until the yolk and white are solid.

SALT: Babies under a year should not have any salt added to their food as this can strain immature kidneys and cause dehydration. A preference for salt can become established at an early age and eating too much salt may lead to high blood pressure later in life. Babies up to six months old should have less than 1g salt a day, and from seven months old they should have a maximum of 1g salt a day. Avoid giving processed foods that are not made specifically for babies, such as pasta sauces and most breakfast cereals, because these can be high in salt. Likewise, smoked foods should be avoided because of their high salt content.

SUGAR: Unless food is really tart, don't add sugar. Adding sugar is habit forming and increases the risk of tooth decay when your baby's first teeth start to come through.

UNPASTEURISED CHEESES, such as Brie, Camembert or Danish Blue, should not be given before twelve months due to the risk of listeria infection.

WHEAT-BASED FOODS and other foods that contain GLUTEN – such as wheat, barley and rye – should not be introduced before six months. When buying baby cereals and rusks before six months, make sure they are gluten-free. Baby rice is the safest type of cereal to try at first.

Cooking Baby Foods

BAKING: If you are cooking something in the oven for the whole family, you could take the opportunity to bake a potato, sweet potato or butternut squash for your baby. Wash and prick the chosen vegetable with a fork and bake in an oven pre-heated to 190°C/375°F/Gas 5 for about 1 hour or until tender. Cut in half, scoop out the flesh and mash together with a little milk and a knob of butter.

BOILING: Use the minimum amount of water – just enough to cover whatever is in the pan – and be careful not to overcook the vegetables or the nutrients they contain will be lost. Add enough of the cooking liquid to the vegetables to make a smooth purée.

MICROWAVING: Chop the vegetables or fruit and place them in a suitable dish. Add a little water, cover, leaving an air vent, and cook on full power until tender. Purée to the desired consistency but take care to stir well and check that it is not too hot to serve to your baby.

STEAMING is the best way to preserve the fresh taste and vitamins in vegetables and fruits. Vitamins B and C are water soluble and can easily be destroyed by overcooking, especially when fruits and vegetables are boiled. Broccoli loses over 60 per cent of its antioxidants when boiled, for instance, but less than 7 per cent when steamed. It's worth buying a multi-layered steamer, which enables you to cook three different vegetables at once. When puréeing vegetables, you can add a little of the boiled water from the bottom of the steamer if the purée is not smooth enough.

STEWING: Put chopped fruit, such as peeled apples or pears, into a thick-based saucepan and, if necessary, add a little water or fruit juice. Cover with a lid and cook over a low heat until tender, then blend the fruit to a purée. Spoon a little into your baby's bowl and serve lukewarm.

Puréeing

During the first few weeks of weaning, it is important that the food you offer your baby is smooth, not too thick and never lumpy.

FOOD PROCESSOR: This is good for puréeing larger quantities such as when making batches of purées for freezing. Many food processors have mini bowl attachments that will serve the purpose better when puréeing smaller quantities. The downside is that they involve more washing up than hand-held electric blenders.

HAND-HELD ELECTRIC BLENDER: This is ideal for making baby purées, especially in very small quantities.

MOULI: This is a food mill that one turns by hand, and it is ideal for puréeing vegetables like potato or sweet potato. A mouli is also good for puréeing foods that have a tough skin, like peas or dried apricots, as you can discard the harder bits. Puréeing potato in a food processor tends to break down the starches and produce a sticky, glutinous pulp, so it is much better to purée it using a mouli.

Freezing food

• Flexible plastic ice-cube trays are ideal for freezing baby food, but make sure that you wrap these in polythene freezer bags. Once frozen, knock out and store the cubes in well-sealed freezer bags and label with the contents and expiry date.

• If you freeze food in ice-cube trays, you can defrost two individual flavours and mix them together to make combinations like apple and pear or sweet potato and parsnip.

• Never refreeze meals that have already been frozen. The exception to this is that raw frozen food can be returned to the freezer once it is cooked. For example, cooked frozen peas can be refrozen.

• Frozen baby purées will keep for six weeks.

• When batch-cooking, cool food as quickly as possible and then freeze it. Don't leave it in the fridge for several days before freezing.

Reheating food

• It is safe to thaw purées in a microwave or saucepan as long as the food is heated all the way through until piping hot. Allow to cool down, and stir thoroughly before giving to your baby.

• Do not reheat food more than once and do not save your baby's half-eaten food as bacteria-carrying saliva from the spoon will have been introduced.

• Your baby's food should be given warm but not too hot as a baby's mouth is more sensitive to heat than an adult's.

• If reheating in a microwave, heat until piping hot and allow to cool. This is to destroy any bacteria that might be present in the food.

• When reheating food in a microwave, stir thoroughly to get rid of any hot spots. Check the temperature before giving to your baby.

Food allergies

The greatest incidence of food allergy occurs in the first few years of life. However, there is no need to be unduly worried about it unless there is a family history of allergy or atopic disease, such as hay fever, asthma or eczema. The incidence of food allergy in most babies is actually very small – about 6 per cent.

A study published in the *Lancet* a couple of years ago found that while 20 per cent of adults in the UK believed that they had some sort of food allergy, IgE testing (which shows whether the allergic response involves the immune system and is therefore a 'true' allergy) revealed that in fact only 3 per cent of those tested did actually suffer from a food allergy.

The commonest foods that carry the risk of allergic reaction in babies are:
• cow's milk and dairy products
• nuts and seeds
• eggs
• wheat-based products
• fish, especially shellfish
• berry and citrus fruits, which can trigger a reaction but rarely cause a true allergy

If one or both parents or a sibling has a history of food allergy or atopic disease, your baby will have an increased risk of developing an allergic disorder, and foods should only be introduced singly and under careful observation. It is best to take the following precautions:

• If possible, breastfeed exclusively for the first six months. If this is not possible, discuss with your doctor the option of using a 'hypoallergenic' infant formula instead.
• When weaning, avoid the high-risk foods listed above, until your baby is at least six months old. Instead start with foods that are unlikely to provoke an allergic reaction, such baby rice, root vegetables, apples or pears.
• New food groups should be introduced one at a time over 2–3 days. In that way, if there is a reaction, you will know what has caused it.
• If there is a history of allergy to a particular food, avoid it until your child is at least six months old.
• If you suspect your child could be allergic to wheat or cow's milk, do not exclude key foods like these from your child's diet without first consulting a doctor.

Although a lot of children grow out of their allergies by the age of three, some allergies – particularly a sensitivity to eggs, milk, fish, shellfish or nuts – can last for life.

What is an allergic reaction?
An allergic reaction generally occurs when the immune system wrongly identifies a harmless substance as a threat and triggers the production of large amounts of antibodies in the blood, which can cause or contribute to various conditions such as eczema, urticaria (itchy red or white raised patches), hay fever, asthma, diarrhoea and even failure to thrive. If your child is found to be allergic to a basic food like wheat or cow's milk, you should seek expert advice on how to keep meals balanced.

Food intolerance
A food intolerance, sometimes referred to as a 'false' food allergy, is a condition whereby the body is incapable of digesting certain foods properly. The condition is generally short-lived and not the same as a true food allergy, which involves the immune system. However, it can provoke the same symptoms, so if you suspect that your child is allergic to a common food like cow's milk, you should consult your paediatrician before changing the milk formula. It is quite possible that your baby's adverse reaction to it is only temporary.

How a food allergy is diagnosed

Food allergy can trigger a wide range of symptoms, from vomiting, itching and swelling in the mouth, throat and skin, to persistent diarrhoea, abdominal pain, eczema, skin rashes and wheezing. With so many symptoms that could have other causes, it is often hard to be sure that food is to blame or to find out which food. Reactions may occur immediately after eating a specific food or may be delayed for hours or even days. If you are worried that your child might be allergic to a certain food, you should seek expert medical advice.

Now that solid foods tend to be introduced from six months – later than before – allergic reactions to foods in young infants is not seen as often as previously was the case. However, it is still babies under the age of eighteen months who are most likely to develop an allergy.

Many people blame food additives, but reactions to these are probably at least a hundred times less common than reactions to natural foods such as milk or wheat.

The only accurate way to diagnose a food allergy is to eliminate the suspected or most common allergens, wait for symptoms to cease and, after a period of up to six weeks, reintroduce them one by one until the symptoms reappear. This type of 'elimination' diet should be done only under medical supervision and with the help of a state-registered dietician. Other methods, such as electrode testing and kinesiology, do not provide an accurate means of diagnosing food allergies.

Allergy to cow's milk protein

This is the most commonly occurring food allergy and affects about 3 per cent of children. An allergic reaction to infant formula or any dairy product can occur in a matter of minutes, or even after a few days. Symptoms can include cramps, diarrhoea, vomiting, a skin rash or breathing difficulties.

If your baby is sensitive to cow's milk-based infant formula, consult your doctor, who should recommend a specially designed hypoallergenic formula, available on prescription. This has quite a distinctive flavour, and whereas breast milk tastes sweet, this can be a little bitter. You may find that your baby may not be keen on this milk if you are still breastfeeding, but persevere; once you have stopped breastfeeding, she should get used to the taste.

Breast milk is the best milk for babies but occasionally breastfeeding mothers may need to eliminate dairy foods from their own diets as these can be transferred to their baby through breast milk. Only do this following the recommendation of your doctor, however.

All dairy products – such as cheese, yoghurt, butter, ice cream and chocolate – must be eliminated from the diet if your child has an allergy to cow's milk protein. In some less severe cases – for example, where cow's milk allergy causes eczema – small amounts of dairy products may be tolerated.

You should only give your baby soya-based infant formula if your GP or health visitor advises you to. In almost all cases, breast milk or another type of formula will be a better choice. Soya based infant milks are not recommended by the Chief Medical Officer for babies under six months due to the high level of phyto-oestrogen, which could pose a risk to the long-term reproductive health of infants. It is probably best to avoid giving infant soya milk to your baby as a main drink for the first year. Also, bear in mind that children under two should not be given standard 'supermarket' soya milk as their main drink – they need a special infant formula as it provides more nutrients.

Because they weigh much less, babies take in a higher proportion of phyto-oestrogen when they drink soya-based infant formula compared with older children who eat some soya products as part of a mixed diet.

You can still use the recipes in this book if your baby has an allergy to cow's milk. Sweetened soya milk and soya margarine make good substitutes for ordinary cow's milk or butter when cooking for your baby. You could also use sunflower margarine, and many soya-based yoghurts and desserts are available. Carob can be substituted for milk chocolate. However, some soya cheeses contain milk traces and therefore may be unsuitable.

If dairy products have to be avoided, it is important to introduce alternative sources of calcium. These can include milk-free cheeses, tofu, leafy green vegetables, dried fruit, seeds, bread and fortified soya drinks.

Lactose intolerance

Lactose is the sugar present in milk. Lactose intolerance is the inability to digest this sugar because of a lack of a digestive enzyme known as lactase in the gut. It is not actually an allergy. The main symptoms are diarrhoea, cramping, flatulence and abdominal distension. Lactose intolerance can be hereditary – where the body simply does not produce sufficient amount of lactase – or it can follow a period of gastroenteritis (infection in the gut). Following gastroenteritis, the sites where the enzyme lactase is produced may be damaged and therefore the lactose remains undigested, causing problems. In a few weeks to months, the enzyme begins to be produced once more and lactose is digested normally again.

Some children may benefit from a milk-free diet for a short period of time. You could give a hydrolysed formula instead, following consultation with your doctor.

When buying food, you need to look out for items that have milk in the ingredients but under a different name – such as casein, caseinates, non-fat milk and whey. Sometimes children who are lactose intolerant are able to tolerate small amounts of hard cheese (with lower levels of lactose) and yoghurts (in which the lactose is digested by bacteria), but this depends very much on the individual child.

Peanut allergy

In the case of peanuts and peanut-based products – which can induce a severe allergic reaction, such as anaphylactic shock, which can be life threatening – it is best to err on the side of caution. In families with a history of any kind of food allergy, it is advisable to avoid all products containing peanuts until the child is three years old and then seek medical advice before introducing them into the diet. Vegetable oils that may contain peanut oil aren't a problem as the oil is refined thereby removing any traces of peanut protein. However, peanut butter and finely ground nuts can be introduced from six months, provided there is no family history of allergy. Whole nuts should not be given to children under the age of five because of the risk of choking.

Eggs

It is usually the protein in egg white that babies are allergic to. Your baby's mouth may swell quickly after being touched by egg, and hives (itchy red or whitish raised patches) are also a common reaction. It is amazing how many foods contain eggs – unless bakery products are labelled with the ingredients, it is always safer to assume that they contain egg. Egg products may also be listed as albumen, lecithin E322, ovoglobulin, globulin, ovalblumen, ovomucin or vitellin. You can buy egg alternatives in the supermarket.

Gluten intolerance

Gluten is found in wheat and other cereals such as rye and barley, and is therefore present in basic foods like bread, pasta, breakfast cereals, cake and biscuits. About 1 per cent of people in Britain suffer from a permanent sensitivity to gluten – what is known as coeliac disease, which is a serious medical condition. If there is a family history of coeliac disease, there is an increased risk that your child will also suffer from it. Symptoms of gluten disease in your child may include loss of appetite, poor growth, swollen abdomen and pale, frothy and smelly stools. The disease is diagnosed medically by a blood test and can be confirmed by actually looking at the gut wall using endoscopy. This needs to be done before wheat is excluded from the diet, otherwise the test may give a false result.

As previously stated, foods containing gluten should not be introduced into any baby's diet before six months. Cereals introduced between 4–6 months should be gluten-free, such as rice or maize. Baby rice is the safest to go for at first. Thereafter, substitute rice, corn noodles or buckwheat spaghetti for wheat pasta, and rice- or corn-based cereals for wheat-based varieties at breakfast. Gluten-free bread, flour, pasta and cakes are also available.

Research shows that most coeliacs can eat moderate portions of oats (for example, a bowl of porridge). Cornflour, white, brown or ground rice or potato flour can be used instead of wheat flour.

Food additives and colourings

Some widely used food additives, like the food colouring tartrazine, have been associated with allergic reactions in a small minority of children. Some links have also been reported between hyperactivity and additives in the diet. There is some evidence that in a small minority additives, such as artificial flavourings and colourings, or natural foods such as milk or wheat, may change behaviour. However, as stated above, this is true of only a very small minority – a much lower incidence than is perceived by parents.

Check the label on dried apricots to make sure they have not been treated with sulphur dioxide (E220). This substance can trigger an asthma attack in a very small number of susceptible babies.

Eczema

Eczema is a complicated subject, and children with eczema should always be examined by their GP. The National Eczema Society (see box) provides information and advice for sufferers. Eczema is often not due to food but to other factors such as clothes detergents, soaps, grass or other pollens in the air. If there is a history of eczema in the family, then breastfeeding may help delay the onset of the condition. The foods most commonly implicated in food allergies that may present as eczema are cow's milk, nuts, wheat, eggs and shellfish.

• Allergy UK is the main charity for allergies in general: tel. 01322 619864, www.allergyuk.org
• For allergy testing, contact tel. 01904 410410, www.yorktest.com
• For information on coeliac disease, contact Coeliac UK, tel. 01494 437278, www.coeliac.co.uk
• For information on eczema, contact the National Eczema Society, tel. 020 7281 3553, www.eczema.org
• For advice on lactose intolerance and links to some great recipes, contact www.lactose.co.uk

Weaning pre-term babies

If your baby was born prematurely, weaning times can vary. Babies born before thirty-seven weeks are considered pre-term and have a greater need for certain nutrients like iron and zinc because these start to be stored in your baby's body in the last months of pregnancy.

A lot of pre-term babies will be ready for solid food before six months' 'corrected' age (i.e. the age of a child calculated from his expected date of delivery). It is advised that pre-term babies be introduced to solids at some point between four and seven months' 'uncorrected' age (i.e. the age of a child calculated from his actual, rather than expected, date of delivery).

There are no particular signs that a baby might show to signal that he is ready to start weaning, and this should be discussed with your health visitor and other health professionals involved in your baby's feeding to ensure that you do not start too early. On the other hand, it seems that making sure lumpy food is not introduced too late may help prevent some feeding difficulties. It has been suggested that babies should be eating food consisting of some soft lumps at least by nine months' uncorrected age. Allowing your baby to have finger foods as soon as he can cope with them will probably also encourage him to accept different foods more readily, as well as helping in the development of eye-to-hand coordination.

In hospital, pre-term babies are usually given breast milk, which can be fortified with protein, vitamins and minerals where necessary. If breast milk is unavailable, they will be given a special infant formula that contains more calories, protein, vitamins and minerals than standard formula milk. Once discharged from hospital, non-breastfed babies are then given a special 'post-discharge' formula like Farleys Premcare or Cow & Gate Nutriprem 2, which is available on prescription and is higher in certain nutrients than standard formula milk. Pre-term babies tend to be in a state of 'catch up' in terms of growth and they often need larger volumes of milk and feeding more frequently than full-term babies.

Care needs to be taken when weaning pre-term babies to ensure that foods are not too low in energy – it is no good filling your baby up with fruit and vegetable purées, thereby displacing the nutrients that his milk provides. Foods like eggs, cheese, Greek yoghurt and avocado are ideal nutrient-dense foods for the second stage of weaning, as are potato- or sweet potato-based purées made with the special formula or breast milk or with a little added butter or olive oil. Baby rice (which is fortified with iron) mixed with the special formula or breast milk is good for breakfast, but try adding some fruit purée to alter the flavour. Contrary to popular belief, babies don't always prefer food that tastes bland.

You also need to ensure that you include foods that provide good sources of protein and iron. Introduce meat at around six months and, a little later, fish. If you don't want to give your baby meat or fish, small amounts of puréed beans or pulses make a good alternative. Offer a wide variety of foods, to ensure a good nutritional balance and discourage your baby from being a fussy eater later on.

First-stage weaning: 6 months

Weaning your baby from milk to solids is an important and exciting milestone for both of you, and it's a big step forward for your baby as it opens up a whole new world of taste.

There is nothing better for your baby than freshly prepared food, and my purée recipes are quick and easy to make. Most are suitable for freezing, so that you don't have to cook them from scratch every day. By making baby food yourself, you can be sure of using only the best-quality ingredients, and homemade purées taste so much better than jars of baby food, which often have a shelf life of up to two years.

Keep to the main guidelines and then follow your instincts because no two babies are the same and Mum usually knows best.

First vegetable purée

350g (12oz) carrots, peeled and chopped

Put the carrots in a steamer set over boiling water and cook for 15–20 minutes until tender. Alternatively, put the carrots in a saucepan and pour over just enough boiling water to cover. Cover with a lid and simmer for 15–20 minutes until soft.

   Drain the carrots and place in a blender, adding some of the water from the bottom of the steamer or some of the cooking liquid, then purée until very smooth. The amount of liquid you add really depends on your baby; you may need to add a little more if he finds the purée difficult to swallow. Spoon some of the purée into your baby's bowl and serve lukewarm.

Food fact: Interestingly, carrots are more nutritious when cooked with a little fat, such as a knob of unsalted butter, as the betacarotene they contain is absorbed more readily.

Carrots make excellent weaning food as babies like their naturally sweet taste.

TOP TIP
It isn't a good idea to delay introducing solids any later than six months. Your baby needs to learn how to chew and swallow food, and learning to chew also encourages the development of the muscles that are essential for speech.

Baby rice should be the first cereal you introduce because it does not contain gluten, a protein that is found in cereals like wheat, barley and rye, and which can cause food allergy if introduced before six months.

TOP TIP
Allow plenty of time for feeding when first introducing solids. Go at your baby's pace. While sucking is a natural reflex, your baby needs to learn to move solid food from the front of the tongue to the back, in order to swallow it.

Creamy vegetable or fruit purée

1 tbsp baby rice
3 tbsp your baby's usual milk
4 tbsp vegetable or fruit purée
(see pages 23 or 25)

Mix the baby rice and milk together according to the instructions on the packet and stir into the vegetable or fruit purée.

First fruit purée

6 MONTHS

MAKES 6 PORTIONS

COOKING TIME: 4–8 MINS

SUITABLE FOR FREEZING

Apples make an easily digested introduction to fruit.

2 medium dessert apples or 2 pears, peeled, cored and chopped
1–2 tbsp water or pure unsweetened apple juice (optional)

Put the chopped fruit into a heavy-based saucepan and, if using apples, add the water or apple juice; ripe pears will not need any extra liquid. Cover with a lid and cook over a low heat until tender (about 6–8 minutes for apples and 4 minutes for pears). Blend the fruit to a purée. Spoon a little into your baby's bowl and serve lukewarm.

Food fact: Apples and pears contain pectin, which can slow things down if your baby has loose stools.

Apple and pear with cinnamon

2 dessert apples
2 ripe pears (such as Conference)
4 tbsp pure unsweetened apple juice or water
generous pinch of ground cinnamon (optional)

Put the fruit into a saucepan together with the apple juice or water and cinnamon (if using), cover with a lid and cook over a low heat for 6–8 minutes until tender. Blend the fruit to a smooth purée.

Apple and pear purée is an ideal first food, being easy to digest and unlikely to cause allergies. Choose sweet apples like the Pink Lady variety or Royal Gala. Some apples like Cox or Granny Smith may have too tart a flavour for your baby.

TOP TIP
Weaning spoons should be sterilised for the first six months. However, once your baby is crawling around and testing objects in her mouth, there is little point in sterilising anything other than bottles and teats. Your baby's bowls can be washed in the dishwasher or very hot water (80°C/176°F).

Broccoli is best steamed or microwaved, as boiling it halves its vitamin C content. If your baby isn't keen on the flavour, mix it with a sweet-tasting vegetable like sweet potato, swede, butternut squash or pumpkin. As a variation on this recipe, try sweet potato and peas or sweet potato and spinach.

Sweet potato and broccoli

200g (7oz) sweet potato, peeled and diced
60g (2½oz) broccoli, cut into florets
15g (½oz) unsalted butter
1–2 tbsp your baby's usual milk

Steam the sweet potato and broccoli until tender (the sweet potato for about 12 minutes; broccoli for 7–8 minutes). Alternatively, place the sweet potato in a saucepan, cover with water and boil for 4 minutes, then add the broccoli and continue to boil for 7–8 minutes. Purée together with the butter and milk.

Butternut squash makes a good combination with vegetables like peas or broccoli and also goes well with fruits like apple or pear.

Butternut squash

450g (1lb) butternut squash, peeled,
cut in half and deseeded
15g (½oz) unsalted butter (optional)
2 tbsp freshly squeezed orange juice (optional)

Chop the butternut squash into pieces and steam or boil for about 12 minutes, then purée. Alternatively, brush each half with melted butter and spoon 1 tbsp orange juice into each cavity. Cover with foil and bake in a pre-heated oven at 180°C/350°F/Gas 4 for 1½ hours or until tender, then blend to a purée.

Food fact: Butternut squash is easily digested, rarely causes allergies and provides a good source of betacarotene, potassium and vitamins C and E.

Trio of root vegetables

200g (7oz) sweet potato, peeled and chopped
200g (7oz) carrots, peeled and chopped
110g (4oz) parsnips, peeled and chopped

Steam the vegetables for about 20 minutes or until tender. Blend to a purée adding a little of the boiled water from the bottom of the steamer (about 75ml/2½fl oz), or some of your baby's usual milk, to make the right consistency for him.

   If you don't have a steamer, put the vegetables into a saucepan and just cover with boiling water. Place a lid on the pan and cook over a medium heat for about 20 minutes until tender. Drain the vegetables and blend to a purée using a little of the cooking liquid or some of your baby's usual milk.

Food fact: Orange-fleshed sweet potato is a good source of vitamin C and betacarotene, and is generally richer in nutrients than ordinary potatoes.

 6 MONTHS

 MAKES 6 PORTIONS

 COOKING TIME: 20 MINS

 SUITABLE FOR FREEZING

Root vegetables have a naturally sweet taste, they purée to a smooth consistency and are unlikely to cause allergies, so they make a good first food. You could substitute sweet potato with another vegetable like swede or pumpkin.

Raw fruits are more nutritious than cooked ones since none of the nutrients are lost. You can combine two different fruits together, as in Avocado or Papaya and Banana (see opposite).

No-cook baby food

Avocado

Cut a small avocado in half, remove the stone, scoop out the flesh and mash together with a little of your baby's usual milk.

Food fact: Avocados are sometimes thought of as a vegetable but they are actually a fruit and contain more nutrients than any other type of fruit. They are a great source of the free-radical-fighting antioxidant vitamin E, which also boosts the immune system. In addition, they are rich in monounsaturated fat, the 'good' type of fat that helps prevent heart disease. The high calorie content of avocados makes them an ideal food for growing babies.

Banana

Peel a small banana and mash with a fork. During the first stages of weaning, add a little of your baby's usual milk, if necessary, to thin down the consistency and provide a familiar taste.

Food fact: Bananas are full of slow-release sugars that provide sustained energy. They are also good for the treatment of both diarrhoea and constipation.

Papaya

Cut a small papaya in half, peel, remove the black seeds and purée or mash the flesh of one half until smooth.

Food fact: Papaya contains papain, an enzyme that breaks down protein and so boosts the digestion, as well as improving indigestion. It is rich in vitamin C and betacarotene. A 75g (3oz) portion of papaya will provide a young child's daily requirement of vitamin C. Papaya is also high in soluble fibre, which is important for normal bowel function.

Avocado or papaya and banana

½ avocado or ½ small papaya
½ small ripe banana, peeled
1–2 tbsp your baby's usual milk

Mash the avocado (peeled and stoned) or papaya (peeled and deseeded) together with the banana and the milk. If using papaya, the milk is then optional.

After first tastes: 6–7 months

Try to wean your baby on to as wide a range of foods as possible.
After first tastes are accepted, you can introduce pretty well all fruit
and vegetables. However, take care with citrus, pineapple, berries and
kiwi fruit as these may upset the stomachs of some susceptible babies.

As well as fruit and vegetable purées, make sure you include foods
that are both nutritious and quite high in calories, such as full-fat
yoghurt or cheese, in your child's diet as babies need these to fuel
their rapid growth.

In addition, it is important to include foods rich in iron, such as
red meat, as iron deficiency is the commonest nutritional deficiency
in babies. As we saw in the Introduction, babies are born with an iron
store that lasts for about six months, and a baby's iron requirements
are particularly high between the ages of six months and two years.
This is a critical time for the growth of the brain, and a lack of iron
in the diet can lead to impaired mental development.

6–7 MONTHS

SEE INDIVIDUAL RECIPES
FOR PORTIONS

COOKING TIMES: SEE
INDIVIDUAL RECIPES

SUITABLE FOR FREEZING

Simple vegetable purées

Broccoli or cauliflower

Place 250g (9oz) small broccoli or cauliflower florets in a steamer and cook for about 10 minutes until tender. Alternatively, put in a pan with enough water to cover, bring to the boil, cover with a lid and simmer for about 6 minutes. Drain and blend to a purée. This works well mixed with potato, carrot or sweet potato. It makes 6 portions.

Corn on the cob

Remove the outer husk and silk from the corn on the cob and rinse well. Cover with boiling water and cook over a medium heat for 10 minutes. Strain and then remove the kernels of corn using a sharp knife. Purée in a mouli. Alternatively, cook 250g (9oz) frozen sweetcorn and then purée. This is good combined with carrot, leek and potato or chicken, leek and potato. It makes 2 portions.

Courgette

Place 250g (9oz) trimmed and sliced courgettes in a steamer and cook for about 10 minutes until tender. Alternatively, put in a pan with enough water to cover, bring to the boil, cover with a lid and simmer for about 6 minutes. Drain and blend to a purée. This makes a good combination with sweet potato, or leek, potato and peas. It makes 8 portions.

Pea

I tend to use frozen peas as they are just as nutritious as the fresh variety. Cover 250g (9oz) peas with water, bring to the boil, cover the pan with a lid and simmer for 4 minutes until tender. (If using fresh peas, cook them for about 15 minutes or until tender.) Drain, reserving some cooking liquid, then purée using a mouli. This purée works well combined with potato, carrot or sweet potato. It makes 2 portions.

Spinach

Carefully wash 110g (4oz) spinach leaves, removing the coarse stalks. Either steam the spinach or put in a saucepan and sprinkle with a little water. Cook for about 3–4 minutes until the leaves are wilted. Gently press out any excess water, then purée in a blender. This works well combined with potato, sweet potato or butternut squash. It makes 1 portion.

Sweet potato, swede or parsnip

Use a large sweet potato, a small swede or 2 parsnips. Scrub, peel and chop into small cubes. Steam the vegetables for about 12 minutes until tender. Alternatively, cover with boiling water and simmer, covered with a lid, for about 15 minutes until tender. Drain, reserving the cooking liquid. Purée in a blender, adding some of the liquid if necessary. This makes 4 portions.

Tomato

Skin, deseed and roughly chop 2 medium tomatoes (see page 125). Melt a knob of unsalted butter in a heavy-bottomed saucepan and sauté the tomato until mushy. Purée in a blender. This is good combined with potato, cauliflower or courgette and a little grated cheese melted into the cooked tomatoes. It makes 1 portion.

6–7 MONTHS

MAKES 1 PORTION

COOKING TIME: NONE

SUITABLE FOR FREEZING
(EXCEPT MELON)

Apricots can be quite
sour, so taste them first
and only give them to
your baby if they are
sweet. Mango, on the
other hand, is naturally
sweet and easy to digest,
but do make sure you
choose a ripe fruit. Galia
and Charentais melons
are also good as they tend
to be naturally sweet.

Simple fruit purées

Fresh apricot

Skin 2 large apricots in the same way as a peach or
nectarine (see page 125), then purée using a hand-held
electric blender. This combines well with banana.

Food fact: Apricots are rich in betacarotene and are a
good source of iron and potassium. Dried apricots are
particularly nutritious as well as being rich in fibre.

Mango

Peel the fruit and slice down each side of the
stone. Cut the flesh of half a mango into cubes
and purée. This combines well with banana,
strawberry or yoghurt.

Food fact: Mango is rich in vitamins A and C.

Melon

Take a small wedge of melon, remove the seeds
and cut the flesh away from the skin, discarding
the greener flesh near the skin. Mash or blend to
a purée of the desired consistency. This purée
combines well with strawberries or banana.

Food fact: Cantaloupe melons are the most nutritious
of all the melon varieties; they are rich in vitamin C
and also provide betacarotene and potassium.

Peach or nectarine

Skin a small, ripe peach or nectarine and chop the flesh (see page 125), then purée in a blender or mash. This purée works well combined with strawberries, banana or blueberries.

Plum

Skin 2 large plums in the same way as a peach or nectarine (see page 125), then chop the flesh. Plums can be puréed uncooked if sufficiently soft and juicy, or you could steam them for a few minutes until tender. They are good mixed with baby rice, banana or yoghurt.

Dried fruit (apricot, peach or prune)

Cover 110g (4oz) fruit with water, bring to the boil and simmer for about 5 minutes until soft. Drain (remove stones from prunes if not pitted) and purée. Add a little of the cooking liquid to make a smooth purée. This can be combined with baby rice and milk, banana, pear or apple purée.

- 6–7 MONTHS
- MAKES 4 PORTIONS
- COOKING TIME: 20 MINS
- SUITABLE FOR FREEZING

Carrots are more nutritious when cooked, unlike many other vegetables. Cooking breaks open the plant cells so that antioxidants and other nutrients can be absorbed more easily by our bodies. It is better to steam swedes rather than boiling them as the vitamin C they contain is water soluble and much of it would be lost in the cooking water.

This would also be good with sweet potato or butternut squash instead of the swede.

Swede, carrot and pea

250g (9oz) swede, peeled and chopped
250g (9oz) carrots, peeled and chopped
75g (3oz) frozen peas

Put the chopped swede and carrots into a steamer and cook for 15 minutes. Alternatively, cover with water in a pan, bring to the boil, cover with a lid and simmer for about 15 minutes. Add the frozen peas and continue to cook for another 5 minutes.

Purée in a blender with as much of the liquid from the bottom of the steamer (or pan) as needed to achieve a smooth consistency. For very young babies, you could purée this in a mouli to get rid of the husks from the peas.

Food facts: Just one large carrot provides the recommended daily intake of vitamin A for an adult. Swedes provide a good source of vitamin C.

See-in-the-dark purée

1 small onion, peeled and sliced
25g (1oz) unsalted butter
450g (1lb) carrots, chopped
350ml (12fl oz) Vegetable or Chicken Stock
(see pages 123 and 124)
60ml (2fl oz) freshly squeezed orange juice

Sauté the onion in the butter until softened. Add the carrots and sauté for 3–4 minutes. Pour over the stock, bring to the boil, then reduce the heat and simmer for about 20 minutes or until the carrots are tender. Add the orange juice and purée in a blender.

Food fact: Carrots do improve night vision. They are an excellent source of betacarotene, the plant form of vitamin A, and one of the first symptoms of vitamin A deficiency is night blindness.

Instead of potato, you could substitute sweet potato, butternut squash or pumpkin in this recipe.

Potato, courgette and pea

50g (2oz) onion, peeled and finely chopped
15g (½oz) unsalted butter
50g (2oz) courgettes, trimmed and thinly sliced
150g (5oz) potatoes, peeled and chopped
125ml (4fl oz) Vegetable or Chicken Stock
(see pages 123 and 124)
25g (1oz) frozen peas

Sauté the onion in the butter for about 3 minutes or until softened. Add the courgettes and sauté for 1 minute. Add the potatoes, pour over the stock, then cover with a lid and simmer for 12 minutes. Tip in the frozen peas, bring to the boil, then reduce the heat and continue to cook for 3 minutes. Purée in a blender.

Food fact: All the yellow-fleshed squashes are good sources of betacarotene, but in courgettes this vitamin is only present in any significant amount in the skin so they are best cooked and eaten with the skin on.

Cinderella's pumpkin

6–7 MONTHS

MAKES 3–4 PORTIONS

COOKING TIME: 32 MINS

SUITABLE FOR FREEZING

15g (½oz) unsalted butter
50g (2oz) white part of a leek, washed and sliced
225g (8oz) pumpkin or butternut squash, peeled
and cut into cubes
150ml (5fl oz) Vegetable or Chicken Stock
(see pages 123 and 124)

Melt the butter in a saucepan and sauté the leek
until soft and lightly golden. Add the pumpkin or
butternut squash and continue to cook for 2 minutes.
Pour over the stock, bring to the boil and then simmer,
covered with a lid, for 30 minutes or until the pumpkin
is tender. Purée in a blender, or mash with a fork
for older babies.

This was one of my youngest daughter's favourite combinations – and it tastes so good you could make it as a soup for the rest of the family. If you can't find pumpkin, try butternut squash instead.

As a meaty variation on this recipe, you could add 60g (2½oz) chopped chicken breast with the pumpkin or butternut squash. Simmer, covered, for 15 rather than 30 minutes.

Sweet potato with spinach and peas

6–7 MONTHS

MAKES 5 PORTIONS

COOKING TIME: 14 MINS

SUITABLE FOR FREEZING

25g (1oz) unsalted butter
50g (2oz) leeks, washed and finely sliced
375g (13oz) sweet potato, peeled and chopped
50g (2oz) frozen peas
75g (3oz) fresh baby spinach, washed
and any tough stalks removed

Melt the butter in a saucepan and sauté the leeks for 2–3 minutes or until softened, then add the sweet potato. Pour over 200ml (7fl oz) water, bring to the boil, then cover with a lid and simmer for 7–8 minutes. Add the peas and spinach and cook for 3 minutes. Purée the vegetables in a blender to make a smooth consistency for your baby, adding a little of the cooking liquid if necessary.

Food fact: Frozen vegetables like peas can be just as nutritious as fresh since they are frozen within hours of being picked, thus locking in vital nutrients. Once cooked, they can be refrozen.

Combining spinach with a sweet-tasting vegetable like sweet potato is a good way to introduce it to your baby. You can also make this recipe with broccoli instead of spinach.

6–7 MONTHS

MAKES 3 PORTIONS

COOKING TIME: 26 MINS

SUITABLE FOR FREEZING

For young babies it is best to purée sweetcorn through a mouli as it will be easier to digest and have a smoother texture.

TOP TIP
Water is the best alternative drink to milk – ideally boiled, cooled tap water. Fully breastfed babies don't need any water until they start eating solid food.

Potato, carrot and sweetcorn

25g (1oz) unsalted butter
50g (2oz) onion, peeled and chopped
175g (6oz) carrots, peeled and chopped
200g (7oz) potatoes, peeled and chopped
250ml (9fl oz) Vegetable Stock (see page 123) or water
50g (2oz) tinned or frozen sweetcorn
1–2 tbsp milk

Melt the butter in a pan and sauté the onion for 1 minute. Add the carrots and sauté for 5 minutes. Tip in the potatoes, cover with the stock or water and cook over a medium heat for 15 minutes. Add the sweetcorn and continue to cook for 5 minutes. Purée through a mouli and stir in the milk to make the right consistency for your baby.

Food fact: Sweetcorn is a good source of beta-carotene and fibre.

This tasty combination of fish and vegetables in a mild cheese sauce is very popular with babies.

TOP TIP
If your child has an allergy or intolerance, make sure you inform everyone who looks after your child.

Fillet of fish with cheese sauce and vegetables

15g (½oz) unsalted butter
50g (2oz) leeks, washed and finely sliced
110g (4oz) carrots, peeled and chopped
250ml (9fl oz) boiling water
50g (2oz) frozen peas
150g (5oz) cod, plaice, hake or haddock fillet, skinned
150ml (5fl oz) milk
3 black peppercorns
1 bay leaf
1 sprig parsley
25g (1oz) unsalted butter
1 tbsp plain flour
50g (2oz) Cheddar cheese, grated

Melt the butter in a saucepan, add the leeks and sauté for 2–3 minutes. Add the carrots, cover with the boiling water and cook for 15 minutes. Add the peas and cook for a further 5 minutes, or until the vegetables are tender.

Meanwhile, put the fish in a pan with the milk, peppercorns, bay leaf and parsley. Simmer for 3–4 minutes or until the fish is cooked. Flake the fish and set aside, reserving the cooking liquid. Discard the flavourings.

Make the cheese sauce (see page 125 for recipe).

Drain the vegetables and mix with the flaked fish and cheese sauce. Blend to a purée of the desired consistency for a young baby. Provided the vegetables are tender, this can be mashed for a younger baby or chopped for one who is beginning to chew.

Chicken with sweet potato and apple

Apple and chicken make a delicious combination. Mixing it with sweet potato gives a smoother texture.

15g (½oz) butter
40g (1½oz) chopped onion
110g (4oz) chicken breast, chopped
300g (11oz) sweet potato, peeled and chopped
½ dessert apple, peeled and chopped
200ml (7fl oz) Chicken Stock (see page 124)

Heat the butter in a saucepan, add the onion and sauté for 2–3 minutes. Add the chicken and sauté for a couple of minutes until it turns opaque. Tip in the sweet potato and apple and pour over the stock. Bring to the boil, then cover with a lid and simmer for 15 minutes. Purée to the desired consistency.

Food fact: Chicken is an ideal 'growth' food as it is packed with protein and vitamin B_{12}, which is not found in plants.

6–7 MONTHS

MAKES I PORTION
(UNLESS OTHERWISE STATED)

COOKING TIME: NONE

UNSUITABLE FOR FREEZING

Some purées are particularly easy to prepare as they use ingredients that don't need to be cooked. Overleaf are some delicious – and very nutritious – combinations for you to try. They are equally suitable for breakfast or dessert and can also be mixed with baby rice. Do make sure that the fruit is sweet and ripe by tasting it first yourself. For the purées with yoghurt, always choose the whole-milk, natural, 'live' variety for babies. Natural Greek-style yoghurt is a good choice too. Fresh peach and dried apricots also go well with yoghurt.

Instant no-cook purées

Bananas (the basis for most of these purées) are a great first food as they are quick to prepare, easy to digest and unlikely to cause an allergic reaction. In addition, they make perfect portable baby food as they come in their own easy-to-peel 'packaging'.

Banana and blueberry

25g (1oz) blueberries
1 small ripe banana, peeled and sliced

Put the blueberries into a saucepan together with 1 tbsp water, and cook for about 2 minutes or until the fruit just starts to burst open. Using a hand-held electric blender, whiz the blueberries and bananas together until smooth.

Banana and mango or papaya

1 small banana, peeled
75g (3oz) mango, peeled and stoned, or papaya, peeled and deseeded

Slice the fruit and blend together.

Banana, peach and strawberry

1 small banana, peeled and sliced
1 ripe peach, skinned and stoned
2 strawberries, hulled and quartered

Blend together all the fruit.

Banana with apple

1 small banana, peeled and sliced
2–3 tbsp apple purée (see page 25)

Simply mash the banana together with the apple purée.

Cantaloupe melon and strawberry

½ ripe Cantaloupe melon, peeled, deseeded and chopped
3 strawberries, hulled and quartered
1–2 tbsp baby rice

Blend the fruit together and stir in the baby rice to thicken the purée.

Banana, avocado and yoghurt

½ small banana, peeled and sliced
½ small ripe avocado
1–2 tbsp natural Greek yoghurt

Mash or purée the banana together with the avocado, and stir in the yoghurt.

Mango and yoghurt

½ small ripe mango, peeled and chopped
3–4 tbsp mild, full-fat natural yogurt

Purée the mango using a hand-held electric blender and mix together with the yoghurt. This makes 2 portions.

Banana and pear

1 small banana, peeled and sliced
½ ripe Conference pear, peeled, cored and chopped

Mash or purée the banana together with the pear.

Note: Purées of banana are best served straight away, otherwise they discolour. Look for little brown spots on the banana skin to make sure it is really ripe.

Banana with tofu

1 small ripe banana
50g (2oz) soft tofu

Peel and mash the banana and mix together with the tofu. You could also mix tofu with other fruits like mango or peaches.

Food fact: Most vegetarians will know the health benefits of tofu, which is made from soya bean curd. It makes an excellent high-protein alternative to meat and is rich in many nutrients, including iron, potassium and calcium.

6–7 MONTHS

MAKES 1 PORTION

COOKING TIME: 2–3 MINS

UNSUITABLE FOR FREEZING

This is a delicious purée to make when sweet, ripe peaches are in season. Their natural sweetness makes them a favourite with little ones.

TOP TIP
It's best not to put anything into a bottle apart from milk or water. Comfort sucking on sweet drinks is the main cause of tooth decay in young children. It is a good idea to start using a lidded cup with a spout from the age of 6–7 months and eventually move on to an open cup.

Peach and banana

1 ripe peach, skinned, stoned and cut into pieces (see page 125)
1 small banana, peeled and sliced
½ tbsp pure apple juice
a little baby rice (optional)

Put the peach and banana into a small pan together with the apple juice, cover with a lid and simmer for 2–3 minutes, then purée in a blender. If the purée is too runny, stir in a little baby rice.

Food fact: Peaches are a good source of vitamin C and easy to digest.

Apple, strawberry and peach

 6–7 MONTHS

 MAKES 4 PORTIONS

 COOKING TIME: 5 MINS

SUITABLE FOR FREEZING

1 large dessert apple, peeled, cored and chopped
1 large peach, peeled, stoned and chopped
(see page 125)
75g (3oz) strawberries, hulled and quartered
1 tbsp baby rice

Put the fruit into a saucepan, cover with a lid and cook over a low heat for about 5 minutes. Purée in a blender and stir in the baby rice.

Food fact: Strawberries contain more vitamin C than other berry fruits and they can help strengthen your child's immune defences. Strawberries also contain ellagic acid, believed to help prevent cancer.

You could finely crush a baby rusk and stir that into the fruit purée instead of the baby rice.

Try also strawberry and peach purée. Peel and chop 2 ripe Conference pears and place in a pan together with 50g (2oz) hulled and quartered strawberries and cook for 3–4 minutes. Purée in a blender and stir in 2 tbsp baby rice to thicken.

6–7 MONTHS

MAKES 12 PORTIONS

COOKING TIME: 34 MINS

SUITABLE FOR FREEZING

This is an ideal purée for introducing young babies to chicken.

Easy one-pot chicken

50g (2oz) leeks, washed and finely sliced
15g (½oz) unsalted butter
110g (4oz) chicken breast, cut into chunks
1 medium carrot, peeled and sliced
275g (10oz) sweet potato, peeled and chopped
300ml (10fl oz) Chicken Stock (see page 124)

Sauté the leeks in the butter until softened. Add the chicken to the pan and sauté for 3–4 minutes. Add the vegetables, pour over the stock, bring to the boil and simmer, covered with a lid, for about 30 minutes or until the chicken is cooked through and the vegetables are tender. Purée in a blender to the desired consistency.

Peach, pear and blueberry

1 ripe, juicy peach, skinned, stoned and chopped (see page 125)
1 medium, ripe pear, peeled, cored and chopped
50g (2oz) blueberries
2–3 tbsp baby rice

Put the fruit into a small saucepan, cover with a lid and cook over a low heat for 3–4 minutes, stirring occasionally. Purée in a blender and stir in the baby rice while still hot.

Food fact: Blueberries are a good source of vitamin C and also contain betacarotene. They have the highest antioxidant content of all fruits, mainly because of the blue pigment, anthocyanin, in their skin.

Soft fruits such as these tend to produce a runny fruit purée – adding baby rice is a good way to thicken the texture.

TOP TIP
Fruit juices are a good source of vitamin C, but bear in mind that giving your baby juices and other drinks will reduce his appetite for milk. Fruit juice is acidic and also contains natural sugars, which can cause tooth decay. It is best not to give your baby fruit juice before he is six months old as some babies can have an adverse reaction to citrus fruit. All fruit juices should be diluted in the proportion of five parts water to one part juice.

Serve this on its own
or mix it with some baby
rice, Greek yoghurt or
mashed banana. Adding
a vanilla pod gives the
fruit a lovely flavour.

Apricot, apple, pear and vanilla

75g (3oz) ready-to-eat dried apricots, chopped
1 large dessert apple, peeled, cored and chopped
1 vanilla pod
4 tbsp pure apple juice or water
1 large ripe pear, peeled, cored and chopped

Put the apricots and apple into a heavy-based
saucepan together with the apple juice or water.
Split the vanilla pod, scrape the seeds into the pan
and throw in the split pod. Bring to the boil, then
cover with a lid and simmer for 3–4 minutes. Add
the chopped pear and continue to simmer for
2 minutes. Remove the vanilla pod. Purée in a blender.

Second-stage weaning: 7–9 Months

Once your baby can sit unsupported, he can use a high chair. Try to make eating a sociable event by getting him to sit at the table with you.

Foods with a thicker consistency and lumpier texture can be introduced to encourage your baby to learn to chew. If he is not hungry at mealtimes, cut down on the amount of milk he drinks so that he is hungrier for his solids and therefore not so fussy about the texture. Your baby should still be having a minimum of 500–600ml (18–20fl oz) milk a day.

Try to give 2–3 servings a day of starchy foods like potatoes, rice, pasta or bread. Fruit and vegetables make good finger foods (see below) and should be included in at least two meals a day. Your baby should have one serving of cooked meat, fish, egg or pulses such as beans or lentils a day. It is important to include red meat in the diet as it is an excellent source of iron. In addition, well-cooked eggs provide an excellent and cheap source of protein, as well as being very easy to prepare.

Once your baby can hold things in his hand, you could also give finger foods, such as:

- peeled apple, pear or banana
- seedless grapes
- dried fruit – raisins or apricots
- steamed or raw vegetables – sticks of carrot or cucumber, broccoli florets
- cubes of cheese
- fingers of toast
- mini sandwiches
- rice cakes

Lentils can be difficult for young babies to digest and should be combined with plenty of fresh vegetables, as in this recipe. You can transform this tasty purée into a delicious soup for the family simply by adding more stock and some seasoning.

TOP TIP
A vegetarian baby's first tastes of food are the same as for other babies – baby rice, fruit and vegetable purées, etc. But from around seven months when proteins are being introduced, it differs. Instead of meat, give dairy foods, eggs and lentils. It's not as easy to absorb iron from non-animal sources, so it's a good idea to give vitamin C-rich fruit or diluted juice to boost iron absorption.

Lovely lentils

50g (2oz) finely chopped onion
100g (4oz) carrots, peeled and chopped
15g (½oz) celery, chopped
1 tbsp vegetable oil
50g (2oz) split red lentils
250g (8oz) sweet potato, peeled and chopped
400ml (14fl oz) Vegetable or Chicken Stock
(see pages 123 and 124) or water

Sauté the onion, carrots and celery in the vegetable oil for about 5 minutes or until softened. Add the lentils and sweet potato to the pan and pour over the water or stock. Bring to the boil, turn down the heat and simmer, covered with a lid, for 20 minutes. Purée in a blender.

Food fact: Lentils are a good, cheap source of protein. They also provide iron, which is very important for brain development, particularly between the ages of six months and two years.

Potatoes blend well with most vegetables. Peel them just before cooking – don't soak them in water beforehand, as they will then lose their vitamin C.

Potato, leek, carrot and pea

25g (1oz) unsalted butter
60g (2½oz) leeks, washed and sliced
175g (6oz) potatoes, peeled and diced
1 medium carrot, peeled and sliced
300ml (10fl oz) Vegetable or Chicken Stock
(see pages 123 and 124)
50g (2oz) frozen peas

Melt the butter in a saucepan and sauté the leeks for 3–4 minutes. Add the potatoes and carrot and pour over the stock. Bring to the boil, then reduce the heat, cover with a lid and cook for 10 minutes. Add the frozen peas and continue to cook for about 6 minutes until the vegetables are tender. Purée in a food processor.

Food fact: Potatoes contain vitamin C and are a good source of potassium.

MAKES 4 PORTIONS

COOKING TIME: 18 MINS

SUITABLE FOR FREEZING

Tomatoes and carrots with basil

125g (4½oz) carrots, peeled and sliced
100g (4oz) cauliflower, cut into florets
25g (1oz) unsalted butter
200g (7oz) ripe tomatoes, skinned, deseeded
and roughly chopped (see page 125)
2–3 fresh basil leaves
50g (2oz) Cheddar cheese, grated

If you introduce your baby to new flavours at an early age, he will tend to grow up a less fussy eater. The sweet/tangy flavours of carrot and tomato in this recipe combine well with the mild-tasting cauliflower.

Put the carrots in a small saucepan, cover with boiling water and simmer, covered with a lid, for 10 minutes. Add the cauliflower and cook, covered, for 7–8 minutes, adding extra water if necessary. Meanwhile, melt the butter in another pan, add the tomatoes and sauté until mushy. Stir in the basil and cheese until melted. Purée the carrots and cauliflower with the tomato sauce and about 3 tbsp of the cooking liquid.

It's a good idea to introduce your child to the flavour of green vegetables early on. Since young babies can find certain vegetables too strong-tasting, you could try mixing these with something milder, such as combining broccoli with potato. You could also make this purée using courgettes instead of the broccoli.

Eat your greens

40g (1½oz) chopped onion
15g (½oz) unsalted butter
250g (9oz) potatoes, peeled and diced
375ml (13fl oz) Vegetable Stock (see page 123) or water
50g (2oz) broccoli, cut into florets
50g (2oz) frozen peas
50g (2oz) fresh spinach, washed

Sauté the onion in the butter for about 5 minutes until softened but not browned. Add the potatoes to the pan and pour over the stock or water. Cover with a lid, bring to the boil and cook for 10 minutes. Add the broccoli florets and cook for 3 minutes, then add the peas and spinach and cook for 3 more minutes. Purée with as much of the cooking liquid as needed to make the desired consistency for your baby.

Mini minestrone

7–9 MONTHS

MAKES 3 PORTIONS

COOKING TIME: 28 MINS

SUITABLE FOR FREEZING

1 tbsp vegetable oil
50g (2oz) diced onion
1 clove garlic, peeled and crushed
75g (3oz) diced carrots
25g (1oz) diced celery
25g (1oz) French beans, topped and
tailed and cut into short lengths
125g (4½oz) diced potatoes
1 tsp tomato purée
250ml (9fl oz) Chicken or Vegetable Stock
(see pages 123 and 124)
2 tbsp small pasta stars
25g (1oz) frozen peas
1 tbsp freshly grated Parmesan cheese

The vegetables in minestrone soup add texture while being sufficiently soft for older babies to chew, as long as they are diced (as here). However, for younger babies you could blend this soup to the desired consistency.

Heat the oil in a saucepan and sauté the onion and garlic for 1 minute. Add the carrots and celery and continue to fry for 5 minutes. Add the French beans, potatoes and tomato purée and cook for 2 minutes. Pour over the stock, bring to the boil and then simmer for 10 minutes. Add the pasta stars and cook for 5 minutes. Finally, add the peas and cook for 5 minutes more. Stir in the cheese. For younger babies, purée in a blender.

It's important to make sure that as well as fruits, vegetables, carbohydrate and protein, babies have enough fat in their diet as this is crucial for growth and development. Babies and young children need proportionately more fat in their diet than do adults. For this reason, dishes like vegetables in a cheese sauce or fruit with Greek yoghurt are ideal for your baby.

Vegetable purée with tomatoes and cheese

200g (7oz) carrots, peeled and chopped
75g (3oz) cauliflower, cut into florets
75g (3oz) courgettes, sliced
15g (½oz) unsalted butter
250g (9oz) ripe tomatoes, skinned, deseeded and chopped (see page 125)
50g (2oz) Cheddar cheese, grated

Put the carrots into a steamer and cook for 10 minutes. If you have a multi-layered steamer, place the cauliflower and courgettes in the basket above the carrots (otherwise mix with the carrots) and continue to cook for 7–8 minutes. If you don't have a steamer, place the carrots in a saucepan, cover with water and boil for 12 minutes. Add the cauliflower and courgettes and continue boiling for 8 minutes.

Melt the butter in a pan, add the chopped tomatoes and sauté them for about 2 minutes until slightly mushy. Stir in the grated cheese until melted. Blend the carrots together with the cauliflower and courgettes, and mix together with the cheese and tomato sauce.

Vegetables with cheese sauce

75g (3oz) cauliflower, cut into florets
50g (2oz) broccoli, cut into florets
1 medium carrot, peeled and sliced
50g (2oz) frozen peas

Cheese sauce
15g (½oz) unsalted butter
15g (½oz) flour
200ml (7fl oz) milk
40g (1½oz) Cheddar cheese, grated

Put the carrot into a steamer set over a pan of boiling water and cook for 8 minutes. Add the broccoli and cook for 5 minutes. Add the frozen peas and continue to cook for 2 minutes. Meanwhile, make the cheese sauce (see page 125).

Pour the sauce over the vegetables and blend to a purée or chop the vegetables for older babies and mix with the sauce. For young babies you can add a little more milk to thin the purée, if necessary. Spoon a little into your baby's bowl and serve lukewarm.

7–9 MONTHS
MAKES 4 PORTIONS
COOKING TIME: 7–10 MINS
SUITABLE FOR FREEZING

If your baby isn't too keen on eating his vegetables, try mixing them with a tasty cheese sauce.

TOP TIP
If you want to bring up your baby on a vegetarian diet, try to ensure that the diet is not too bulky – don't give too many high-fibre cereals and foods like lentils. Make sure that you provide plenty of highly calorific, nutrient-dense foods like cheese and eggs.

For the cheese sauce, you can experiment using different mild cheeses, like Edam or Emmental. You could also mix in other vegetables, like carrots or spinach.

Cauliflower and broccoli in cheese sauce

110g (4oz) cauliflower, cut into florets
50g (2oz) broccoli, cut into florets
20g (¾oz) unsalted butter
20g (¾oz) flour
200ml (7fl oz) milk
pinch of nutmeg
25g (1oz) Cheddar cheese, grated
25g (1oz) Gruyère cheese, grated

Steam the cauliflower and broccoli for about 7 minutes until tender (or boil in a saucepan of water for 7 minutes until tender). Meanwhile, prepare the cheese sauce as on page 125, adding the nutmeg with the milk and adding both cheeses to the sauce. Purée in a blender for babies under nine months. For older babies able to chew, chop the cauliflower and broccoli into small pieces and mix with the cheese sauce.

7–9 MONTHS

MAKES 2 PORTIONS

COOKING TIME: 10 MINS

SUITABLE FOR FREEZING

Butternut squash is very popular with young babies because of its smooth texture and naturally sweet taste.

Pasta with butternut squash, tomatoes and cheese

200g (7oz) butternut squash, chopped
1½ tbsp tiny pasta stars
15g (½oz) unsalted butter
150g (5oz) tomatoes, skinned, deseeded and chopped (see page 125)
20g (¾oz) Cheddar cheese, grated
2 tbsp milk

Steam or boil the butternut squash for 10 minutes or until tender. Meanwhile, cook the pasta stars according to the instructions on the packet, but without adding salt to the water. Melt the butter in a small saucepan and sauté the tomatoes until mushy, then stir in the cheese until melted. Blend the cooked butternut squash and tomato and cheese mixture together with the milk using a hand-held electric blender, and stir in the pasta stars.

7–9 MONTHS

MAKES 5 PORTIONS

COOKING TIME: 20 MINS

SUITABLE FOR FREEZING

This is one of my family's favourite fish recipes. Do not be put off by the odd-sounding combination, as it gives a marvellously rich taste.

Fillet of fish in an orange sauce

225g (8oz) fillet of fish (such as cod, haddock or hake), skinned
125ml (4fl oz) freshly squeezed orange juice
40g (1½oz) Cheddar cheese, grated
1 dessertspoon finely chopped fresh parsley
25g (1oz) crushed cornflakes
15g (½oz) unsalted butter

Put the haddock in a greased dish, cover with the orange juice, cheese, parsley and cornflakes and dot with the butter. Cover with foil and bake at 180°C/350°F/Gas 4 for about 20 minutes. Alternatively, cover with a lid and cook in a microwave on high for 4 minutes. Flake the fish carefully, removing any bones, and mash everything together with the liquid in which the fish was cooked.

Plaice is one of the best fish to start with as it has a suitably soft texture for young babies.

Fillet of plaice with carrots, cheese and tomatoes

250g (9oz) carrots, peeled and sliced
225g (8oz) plaice fillets, skinned
2 tbsp milk
40g (1½oz) unsalted butter
2 ripe tomatoes, skinned, deseeded and chopped
(see page 125)
40g (1½oz) Cheddar cheese, grated

Put the carrots in a steamer set over a pan of boiling water and cook for 20 minutes. Meanwhile, place the fish in a microwave dish, add the milk, dot with 15g (½oz) butter and cover, leaving an air vent. Microwave on high for 2–3 minutes. Alternatively, put the fish in a pan, cover with a little milk and simmer for about 5 minutes, or until cooked.

Melt the remaining butter in a saucepan, add the tomatoes and sauté until mushy. Stir in the cheese until melted. Blend the carrots with the tomato mixture. Remove the fish from its cooking liquor and flake, making sure there are no bones. Mix the fish with the carrots and tomatoes. For younger babies you can blend the fish together with the carrots and tomato for a smoother texture.

Salmon surprise

200g (7oz) carrots, peeled and sliced
125g (4½oz) salmon fillet, skinned
60ml (2fl oz) orange juice
40g (1½oz) Cheddar cheese, grated
15g (½oz) unsalted butter
2 tbsp milk

 7–9 MONTHS

 MAKES 3 PORTIONS

 COOKING TIME: 20 MINS

❄ SUITABLE FOR FREEZING

Like the previous recipe, this also uses the delicious, if slightly unusual, combination of fish and orange.

Put the carrots into a saucepan, cover with water, bring to the boil and cook over a medium heat for about 20 minutes until tender. Alternatively, place the vegetables in a steamer and cook for 20 minutes.

Meanwhile, place the salmon in a suitable dish, pour over the orange juice and scatter over the cheese. Cover, leaving an air vent, and microwave on high for about 2 minutes or until the fish flakes easily with a fork. Alternatively, cover with foil and cook in the oven, pre-heated to 180°C/350°F/Gas 4, for about 20 minutes.

Flake the fish with a fork, carefully removing any bones. Drain the carrots, mix with the butter and milk, and purée in a blender together with the flaked fish and its sauce. For older babies, mash the carrots together with the butter and the milk and then mix the flaked fish with the mashed carrots.

Food fact: Oily fish like salmon provides a good source of essential fatty acids that are important for development of the brain and eyes.

Babies love the sweet taste of sweetcorn. The trouble is, when it is made into a purée the husks tend to be a bit lumpy and difficult to digest, so for young babies I prefer to put it through a mouli. For older babies, I purée the potato mixture and then stir in the sweetcorn whole.

Cherub's chowder

1 onion, peeled and chopped
1 tbsp vegetable oil
225g (8oz) potatoes, peeled and diced
175ml (6fl oz) Vegetable or Chicken Stock
(see pages 123 and 124)
50g (2oz) fresh or frozen sweetcorn
60ml (2fl oz) milk
50g (2oz) cooked chicken, diced

Sauté the chopped onion in the oil until soft. Add the potatoes to the pan and pour over the stock. Bring to the boil, then cover with a lid and simmer for about 12 minutes. Add the sweetcorn and the milk and simmer for a further 2–3 minutes. Purée the soup in a mouli, together with the chicken, and heat through. Alternatively, for older babies, purée the onion and potato mixture in a mouli, then stir in the sweetcorn whole and the finely chopped chicken. Add a little extra milk and stock to make this into soup.

Chicken liver with vegetables and apple

7–9 MONTHS

MAKES 5 PORTIONS

COOKING TIME: 23 MINS

SUITABLE FOR FREEZING

100g (4oz) chicken livers
40g (1½oz) chopped onion
1 tbsp vegetable oil
1 medium carrot, peeled and sliced
1 large potato, peeled and diced
½ small dessert apple, peeled, cored and chopped
250ml (8fl oz) Chicken Stock (see page 124)

Clean the livers, removing any fat or gristle, and slice them. Sauté the onion in the vegetable oil until softened. Add the sliced liver and sauté for about 1 minute until it has changed colour. Add the carrot, potato and apple, pour over the stock and simmer for 20 minutes. Purée in a food processor.

Food fact: Chicken liver provides a good source of vitamins and iron. Babies are born with a store of iron that lasts for about six months, so after this time it is important to ensure they get all the iron that they need from their diet.

TOP TIP
When teething, your baby may lose his appetite. Rubbing a teething gel on to his gums may help ease the pain. It can also be soothing for your baby to chew on something cool like a chilled cucumber stick.

Since the dark meat of a chicken is even more nutritious than the breast, and tends to be moister, it's a good idea sometimes to use the thighs instead.

Chicken with leeks, carrots and peas

½ tbsp vegetable oil
50g (2oz) leeks, washed and chopped
1 large chicken thigh on the bone (about 175g/6oz),
skinned and trimmed of fat
200g (7oz) carrots, peeled and chopped
250ml (9fl oz) Chicken Stock (see page 124)
50g (2oz) frozen peas

Heat the oil in a saucepan and sauté the leeks for 2 minutes. Add the chicken and sauté for about 2 minutes. Tip in the carrots and pour over the stock, then bring to the boil, cover with a lid and simmer for 20 minutes. Add the peas and cook uncovered for 4–5 minutes. Remove the chicken with a slotted spoon and take the flesh off the bone. Blend together the vegetables and chicken with as much of the cooking liquid as necessary to make a smooth purée.

Beef needs long,
slow cooking to make
it really tender.

My first beef casserole

1½ tbsp vegetable oil
1 onion, peeled and finely chopped
1 clove garlic, peeled and crushed
1½ tbsp flour
1 tsp paprika
300g (11oz) lean stewing steak
400ml (14fl oz) Chicken Stock (see page 124) or water
200g (7 oz) carrots, peeled and chopped
300g (11oz) potatoes, peeled and chopped
½ stick celery, trimmed and chopped
sprig of parsley
sprig of thyme (optional)
110g (4oz) button mushrooms, wiped and sliced

Pre-heat the oven to 150°C/300°F/Gas 2. Heat the oil in a casserole dish and sauté the onion and garlic for 3 minutes. Mix the flour and paprika together in a small bowl and toss the meat in this to coat it. Add the floured meat to the pan and sauté until browned all over.

Pour in the stock or water and stir for 1 minute. Add the vegetables and herbs, then cover and cook in the pre-heated oven for 2 hours. Add the mushrooms and continue to cook for 30 minutes. Purée in a blender.

💡 Food fact: Red meat provides the richest source of iron, which is essential for your baby's physical and mental development.

Braised beef with carrot, parsnip and sweet potato

7–9 MONTHS

MAKES 5 PORTIONS

COOKING TIME:
1 HOUR 50 MINS

SUITABLE FOR FREEZING

1 tbsp olive oil
75g (3oz) chopped red onion
1 clove garlic, peeled and crushed
150g (5oz) lean braising steak, cut into pieces
2 tbsp flour
150g (5oz) carrots, peeled and sliced
75g (3oz) parsnips, peeled and sliced
250g (9oz) sweet potato, peeled and chopped
1 bay leaf
1 tbsp chopped fresh parsley
400ml (14fl oz) Chicken Stock (see page 124)

This recipe makes a good introduction to red meat. Sometimes babies don't like to eat it because they find it too difficult to chew. In this recipe, I have mixed the meat together with root vegetables to give the meat a smooth texture and a flavour that will appeal to babies.

Heat the oil in a heavy-bottomed saucepan or small casserole dish. Sauté the onion and garlic for 3–4 minutes until softened. Toss the pieces of steak in the flour and sauté until browned all over. Add the carrots, parsnips, sweet potato, bay leaf and parsley to the pan and pour over the stock. Bring to the boil and then simmer, covered with a lid, for about 1¾ hours or until the meat is tender. Blend, adding as much of the cooking liquid as necessary.

7–9 MONTHS

MAKES 3 PORTIONS

COOKING TIME:
55 MINS – 1 HOUR

SUITABLE FOR FREEZING

Lamb tends to be quite popular with young babies, and combining lamb with sweet potato gives it a nice soft texture.

Sweet potato and lamb casserole

1 lamb cutlet (about 90g/3½oz in weight), trimmed of fat and diced
2 spring onions, thinly sliced
275g (10oz) sweet potato, peeled and chopped
75g (3oz) tomatoes, skinned, deseeded and chopped (see page 125)
pinch of dried rosemary or mixed herbs
125ml (4fl oz) Chicken Stock (see page 125)

Pre-heat the oven to 180°C/350°F/Gas 4. Put all the ingredients into a small casserole dish, cover with a lid and cook in the oven for 10–15 minutes until bubbling. Reduce the heat to 150°C/300°F/Gas 2 and continue to cook for about 45 minutes or until the lamb is tender. Blend to a purée or chop into small pieces for older babies.

Food fact: Lamb provides a good source of B vitamins, zinc and iron.

Baby muesli

4 tbsp rolled oats
6 tbsp milk
2 small eating apples (approx. 130g each), peeled,
cored and chopped
1 small ripe pear, peeled, cored and chopped
2 tbsp apple juice or water
2 tbsp raisins

Soak the oats in the milk overnight or for at least a
couple of hours. Put the chopped apple and pear in a
saucepan with the apple juice or water. Cover and cook
for 8–10 minutes over a low heat. Remove from the
heat and mash with a fork. Stir into the soaked oats
along with the raisins. Add more fruit purée to taste.

 FROM 7 MONTHS

MAKES 2 PORTIONS

COOKING TIME: 10 MINS

UNSUITABLE FOR FREEZING

This tasty and nutritious
breakfast will make a good
start to the day for your baby.
You could also make this
using chopped dried apricots
instead of raisins. It's a good
idea to make up a batch of
apple and pear purée and
freeze it in ice cube trays.

Ready Brek with banana

100ml (3½fl oz) milk
3 tbsp Ready Brek
1 small banana, peeled
1 tsp maple syrup or a sprinkling of brown sugar

Bring the milk to the boil in a small saucepan. Stir
in the Ready Brek and cook over a gentle heat until
thickened. Mash the banana and stir into the Ready
Brek, together with the maple syrup or sugar.

 7–9 MONTHS

 MAKES 1 PORTION

 COOKING TIME: 5 MINS

UNSUITABLE FOR FREEZING

You don't need to give
only special baby cereals
to your child, provided they
contain less than 1g salt.
You could crush a Weetabix,
for instance, mixing it with
75ml (2½fl oz) milk and
a small mashed banana.

This was my children's favourite breakfast when they were babies. Not only does it taste great, it is also packed full of nutritious ingredients.

TOP TIP
Your baby may start grabbing the spoon you use to feed her, so it's a good idea to give her a second, identical spoon to hold while you feed her. Once she can get the spoon into her mouth, try giving food that will stick to the spoon, like porridge.

My favourite porridge

150ml (5fl oz) milk
15g (½oz) porridge oats
6 ready-to-eat dried apricots, chopped
1 large ripe pear, peeled, cored and chopped

Put the milk, porridge oats and chopped apricots into a small saucepan, bring to the boil and then simmer, stirring occasionally, for 3 minutes. Purée with the chopped pear using a hand-held electric blender.

You could also make this recipe using soft, ready-to-eat dried figs instead of prunes.

Apple, pear and prunes with oats

2 tbsp porridge oats
4 tbsp pure, unsweetened apple juice
2 tbsp water
1 small dessert apple, peeled, cored and chopped
2 stoned prunes, chopped
1 small ripe pear, peeled, cored and chopped

Put the oats, apple juice and water in a saucepan, bring to the boil and simmer for 2 minutes. Add the apple, prunes and pear, cover with a lid and simmer for 3 minutes, stirring occasionally. Purée to the desired consistency.

Food fact: Prunes are a good source of instant energy, fibre and iron. They help with constipation as they are a natural laxative.

This purée takes just minutes to prepare and tastes delicious.

Apricot and banana custard

50g (2oz) ready-to-eat dried apricots, roughly chopped
90ml (3fl oz) boiling water
1 small ripe banana, peeled and sliced
1 tbsp custard powder

Put the apricots into a small saucepan, pour over half the water and simmer for 2–3 minutes. Blend the apricots and cooking liquid together with the banana. Put the custard powder in a small saucepan and mix in a little of the boiling water to make a paste. Pour over the rest of the boiling water and stir briskly over a medium heat until smooth and creamy. Mix the custard together with the apricot and banana purée.

Food fact: Dried apricots are one of nature's superfoods. The drying process increases their concentration of betacarotene, potassium and iron.

In the summer when cherries are deliciously sweet, it's nice to be able to give them to your baby.

Banana and cherry

6 sweet cherries, halved and stoned
1 tbsp water
1 ripe banana, peeled
1 tbsp baby rice

Put the cherries into a small pan together with the water and simmer for 2 minutes. Mash the banana, add to the cooked cherries and simmer for just under a minute. Purée using a hand-held electric blender and stir in the baby rice.

Food fact: Cherries stimulate the immune system and help to prevent infection. They are also good for a child suffering from constipation.

Blueberry, banana and apple

110g (4oz) blueberries
1 small banana, peeled and sliced
1 small dessert apple, peeled, cored and chopped

Put all the fruit into a heavy-bottomed pan and cook, covered with a lid, over a gentle heat for 5 minutes. Remove the lid and simmer for 5 minutes more or until most of the juices have evaporated.

7–9 MONTHS
MAKES 3 PORTIONS
COOKING TIME: 10 MINS
UNSUITABLE FOR FREEZING

Strawberry, peach and pear crumble

75g (3 oz) strawberries, hulled and quartered
1 large, juicy ripe peach, skinned, stoned and cut into pieces (see page 125)
1 large ripe pear, peeled, cored and cut into pieces
1 baby rusk

Put the fruit into a small, heavy-based saucepan, cover with a lid and simmer for about 3 minutes. Crush the rusk (place in a plastic bag and crush with a rolling pin), then blend the fruit together with the crushed rusk.

7–9 MONTHS
MAKES 2 PORTIONS
COOKING TIME: 3 MINS
SUITABLE FOR FREEZING

Some fruit purées are very runny, but you can thicken them by stirring in some baby rice, mashed banana or crumbled rusk, as here. You could also make this with 2 peaches instead of the pear.

Growing independence: 9–12 months

The final quarter of a baby's year is a period of rapid change. She will progress from sitting to crawling and maybe even walking. This is a time of growing independence and you may find that your baby will increasingly insist on feeding herself.

Offer finger foods as part of her meals to give chewing practice and encourage her to feed herself if she is not doing so already. Give steamed or raw vegetable sticks or fresh fruit with a favourite fruit purée as a dip. See also page 63 for other suggestions.

Her diet can now include virtually all the same foods as the rest of the family, apart from added salt, lightly cooked eggs, unpasteurised cheeses, low-fat or high-fibre products, whole nuts and honey.

If your baby is on the move, you may need to increase the amount of food you give to her. Make sure her diet includes full-fat dairy products, in addition to fruit and vegetables, and nutrient-dense foods like Tuna Pasta with Creamy Tomato Sauce or Risotto with Butternut Squash (pages 109 and 100). Babies only have small stomachs and so need to be fed at regular intervals.

Try to dispense with bottles by the time your baby is a year old, apart from perhaps one at bedtime. Encourage your baby to drink from a cup or beaker – it is better for her teeth.

Eggs are quick to prepare but must be cooked through; raw or lightly cooked eggs should not be given to babies or young children because of the risk of salmonella. For babies under one year, the white and yolk should be cooked until solid. You could add some chopped tomato to the scrambled egg if you like.

Scrambled egg with cheese

2 eggs
1 tbsp milk
2 tbsp grated Cheddar cheese
15g (½oz) unsalted butter

Whisk together the eggs, milk and cheese. Melt the butter in a small pan, add the egg mixture and then cook over a gentle heat for 2–3 minutes, stirring, until the mixture sets.

Food fact: Eggs provide protein, vitamins and minerals, while egg yolk offers a good source of iron for your baby.

Carrot, cheese and tomato risotto

40g (1½oz) chopped onion
25g (1oz) unsalted butter
100g (4oz) long grain rice
150g (5oz) carrots, peeled and sliced
300ml (10fl oz) boiling water
3 ripe tomatoes (approx. 200g/7oz), skinned, deseeded
and chopped (see page 126)
50g (2oz) grated Cheddar cheese

Sauté the onion in half the butter until softened. Stir in the rice until well coated, then add the carrots. Pour over the boiling water, bring back to the boil, then cover the pan with a lid and simmer for 15–20 minutes until the rice is cooked and the carrots are tender. If necessary, top up with extra water.

Meanwhile, melt the remaining butter in a small pan, add the tomatoes and sauté for 2–3 minutes until mushy. Stir in the cheese until melted. The water from the rice should have been absorbed but, if not, drain off any excess. Stir the tomato and cheese mixture into the cooked rice.

This dish is both nutritious and very easy to prepare. Cooked rice is soft and so it is a good way of introducing texture to your baby's food. Babies and toddlers tend to like rice and carrots, and here I have flavoured them with sautéed tomatoes and melted cheese for a very tasty meal.

TOP TIP
Surveys have shown that 1 in every 5 babies aged 10–12 months has daily intakes of iron below the recommended level.

Serving cooked rice with vegetables is an ideal way to introduce texture to your baby's food. Butternut squash is now more readily available in supermarkets, although you could substitute it with pumpkin instead.

TOP TIP
The more you allow your baby to experiment using a spoon, the quicker she will learn to feed herself.

Risotto with butternut squash

50g (2oz) onion, chopped
25g (1oz) unsalted butter
110g (4oz) basmati rice
450ml (16fl oz) boiling water
150g (5oz) butternut squash, peeled and chopped
225g (8oz) ripe tomatoes, skinned, deseeded and chopped (see page 125)
50g (2oz) Cheddar cheese, grated

Sauté the onion in half the butter until softened. Stir in the rice until well coated. Pour over the boiling water, cover the pan with a lid and cook for 8 minutes over a high heat. Stir in the butternut squash, reduce the heat and cook, covered, for about 12 minutes or until the water has been absorbed.

Meanwhile, melt the remaining butter in a small saucepan, add the tomatoes and sauté for 2–3 minutes. Stir in the cheese until melted, then stir the tomato and cheese mixture into the cooked rice.

9–12 MONTHS

 MAKES 4 PORTIONS

 COOKING TIME: 12 MINS

 SUITABLE FOR FREEZING

Pasta is a great energy food. Orzo are tiny pasta shapes that look like rice, but if you can't find them you could use any other small pasta shapes instead. You can vary the vegetables, if you like, using peas and sweetcorn instead of the courgettes and broccoli, and adding diced tomatoes with the cheese.

Pasta risotto

75g (3oz) orzo or other small pasta shapes
50g (2oz) carrots, peeled and diced
50g (2oz) courgettes, washed and diced
50g (2oz) broccoli florets, chopped
25g (1oz) unsalted butter
25g (1oz) Cheddar cheese, grated

Put the pasta in a saucepan together with the carrots, cover generously with boiling water and cook for 5 minutes. Add the courgettes and broccoli and continue to cook for about 7 minutes. Melt the butter in a saucepan, stir in the drained pasta and vegetables and toss with the butter and Cheddar until the cheese has melted.

Adding tiny pasta shapes to purées introduces texture in a gradual way. This tasty sauce is also very nutritious.

Pasta stars with tasty vegetable sauce

1 tbsp olive oil
50g (2oz) chopped onion
1 clove garlic, peeled and crushed
150g (5oz) carrots, peeled and chopped
40g (1½oz) red pepper
200g (7oz) tinned chopped tomatoes (or ½ x 400g can)
200ml (7fl oz) water
25g (1oz) frozen peas
3 tbsp tiny pasta stars
40g (1½oz) Cheddar cheese, grated

Heat the oil in a saucepan and sauté the onion and garlic for 1 minute. Add the carrots and red pepper and continue to cook for 5 minutes. Add the tomatoes and water. Bring to the boil, then cover with a lid and simmer for 15 minutes.

Meanwhile, cook the pasta stars according to the instructions on the packet, but without adding salt to the water. Add the peas to the tomatoes and vegetables and continue to cook for 5 minutes. Remove from the heat and stir in the grated cheese until melted. Blend the mixture to a purée. Drain the pasta and stir into the sauce.

Food fact: Tomatoes are rich in lycopene, a powerful antioxidant that helps to protect against heart disease and cancer.

Mashed potato and carrot with broccoli and cheese

300g (11oz) potatoes, peeled and chopped
125g (4½oz) carrots, peeled and sliced
75g (3oz) broccoli, cut into florets
2 tbsp milk
15g (½oz) unsalted butter
40g (1½oz) Cheddar cheese, grated

Put the potatoes and carrots into a saucepan, cover with boiling water and cook for about 20 minutes until tender. Meanwhile, steam the broccoli for 7–8 minutes until tender. Alternatively, add to the potatoes and carrots after about 12 minutes and continue cooking for 7–8 minutes. Drain the potatoes and carrots and mash together with the broccoli, milk, butter and cheese.

 9–12 MONTHS

 MAKES 4 PORTIONS

 COOKING TIME: 20 MINS

 SUITABLE FOR FREEZING

Mashing rather than puréeing your baby's food is a good way to gradually introduce more texture. The relatively strong flavour of the broccoli is toned down by the creamy mashed potato and cheese.

TOP TIP
Bowls that stick to the tray of the high chair with suction are a good idea as it makes it easier for your baby to get food on to his spoon without the bowl moving around on the tray.

This is a great way to get children to eat vegetables because they are blended into the sauce to make them invisible, and what they can't see, they can't pick out. For a creamier version, you can stir in a little mascarpone (an Italian cream cheese).

Pasta with hidden vegetables

2 tbsp light olive oil
1 small onion, peeled and chopped
1 clove garlic, peeled and crushed
75g (3oz) carrots, peeled and chopped
75g (3oz) courgettes, trimmed and chopped
75g (3oz) button mushrooms, wiped and chopped
200g (7oz) ripe plum tomatoes, peeled, deseeded and chopped (see page 125)
15g (½oz) unsalted butter
1 x 400g can chopped tomatoes
100ml (3½fl oz) Vegetable Stock (see page 123)
¼ tsp brown sugar
1 tbsp torn fresh basil leaves
freshly ground black pepper
250g pasta shapes
3–4 tbsp mascarpone cheese (optional)

Heat the oil in a saucepan, add the onion and garlic and sauté for about 3 minutes. Add the carrots and sauté for 4–5 minutes. Tip in the courgettes and sauté for 2 minutes, followed by the mushrooms, sautéing for 2 minutes.

Add the fresh tomatoes and the butter and sauté for 2 minutes. Pour in the can of tomatoes and half the juice. Finally, add the stock, sugar and basil and season with pepper to taste. Cover and cook over a medium heat for 10 minutes, then blend to a purée.

Meanwhile, cook the pasta according to the packet instructions until tender, but without adding any salt. Toss the cooked pasta with the sauce.

Spinach is a good source of betacarotene and vitamin C, so try not to overcook it or you will destroy a lot of its vitamin content.

TOP TIP
If your baby is constipated, give foods that are naturally rich in fibre, like prunes, cooked pears, mashed papaya, lentils and wholegrain cereals. Stop giving rice cereal or banana, and increase fluids wherever possible, in the form of breast milk, water or diluted juice.

Fillet of cod with spinach in a cheese sauce

200g (7oz) cod fillet, skinned
15g (½oz) unsalted butter
½ lemon
110g (4oz) fresh spinach, carefully washed

Cheese sauce
15g (½oz) unsalted butter
1 tbsp flour
175ml (6fl oz) milk
pinch of freshly grated nutmeg
40g (1½oz) Cheddar cheese, grated

Put the fish in a suitable dish, dot with the butter and add a squeeze of lemon juice. Cover, leaving an air vent, and microwave on high for 3–4 minutes until the fish flakes easily with a fork. Alternatively, you can poach the fish in the milk (for the cheese sauce) with a bay leaf, parsley stalk and a few peppercorns for 3–4 minutes, then strain the milk and use to make the cheese sauce.

Cook the spinach in a saucepan with just a little water clinging to the leaves for about 2 minutes or until wilted, and squeeze out any excess liquid. To make the cheese sauce, follow the instructions on page 125, adding the nutmeg with the milk. Flake the cooked fish, chop the spinach and mix with the cheese sauce.

Tuna pasta with creamy tomato sauce

40g (1½oz) small pasta shapes
40g (1½oz) finely chopped onion
1 clove garlic, peeled and crushed
1 tbsp vegetable oil
150ml (5fl oz) passata
1 x 200g can tuna in oil, drained and flaked

Cheese sauce
15g (½oz) unsalted butter
1 tbsp flour
150ml (5fl oz) milk
25g (1oz) Cheddar cheese, grated

Cook the pasta according to the packet instructions, but without adding salt to the water. To make the cheese sauce, follow the instructions on page 126. Meanwhile, sauté the onion and garlic in the oil until softened, stir in the passata and flaked tuna and cook for about 4 minutes. Mix the cheese sauce with the tuna and tomato and stir in the cooked pasta.

Food fact: Tuna provides an excellent source of protein and vitamins, especially D and B$_{12}$. However, unlike fresh tuna, canned tuna does not contain omega-3 essential fatty acids.

9–12 MONTHS

MAKES 3 PORTIONS

COOKING TIME: 12 MINS

SUITABLE FOR FREEZING

Tinned tuna is so nutritious and such a great store-cupboard standby that it's good to encourage a liking for it at an early age.

Mixing soft cooked rice or small pasta shapes into your baby's purée is a good way to introduce texture.

Chicken with tomatoes and rice

1 tbsp olive oil
50g (2oz) chopped onion
1 small clove garlic, peeled and crushed
75g (3oz) chicken breast, cut into chunks
175g (6oz) carrots, peeled and chopped
125g (5oz) potatoes, peeled and chopped
½ x 400g can chopped tomatoes
1 sprig thyme (optional)
150ml (5fl oz) Chicken Stock (see page 124) or water
60ml (2fl oz) pure apple juice
50g (2oz) cooked rice

Heat the oil in a heavy-bottomed saucepan and sauté the onion and garlic for about 4 minutes until softened but not browned. Add the chicken and sauté for about 2 minutes until sealed. Add the carrots, potatoes, tomatoes and thyme (if using) and pour over the stock or water, plus the apple juice. Bring to the boil, then cover with a lid and simmer for 20 minutes.

Remove the thyme. Blitz the chicken and vegetables to the desired consistency in a blender, then mix in the cooked rice.

Tasty chicken Bolognese

9–12 MONTHS

MAKES 2 PORTIONS

COOKING TIME: 24 MINS

SUITABLE FOR FREEZING

1 tbsp olive oil
1 small onion, peeled and chopped
1 clove garlic, peeled and crushed
50g (2oz) carrots, peeled and grated
150g (5oz) minced chicken or turkey
½ tsp fresh thyme leaves or a pinch of dried thyme
150ml (5fl oz) passata
150ml (5fl oz) Chicken Stock (see page 124)
25g (1oz) spaghetti

This delicious sauce can be mixed with any type of pasta. As your baby gets older, you will probably find that you don't need to purée the sauce.

Heat the oil in a saucepan, add the onion and garlic and sauté for 3 minutes, stirring occasionally. Add the carrots and continue to cook for 3 minutes. Tip in the chicken and cook, stirring occasionally, for about 3 minutes. Add the thyme, passata and stock, bring to the boil and then simmer, covered with a lid, for 15 minutes.

Meanwhile, cook the spaghetti according to the instructions on the packet, without adding any salt. Drain and chop into small pieces. Using a hand-held electric blender, whizz the Bolognese sauce for a few seconds to make a smoother texture and then stir in the chopped spaghetti.

Chicken is a good source of lean protein as well as having a suitably soft texture for your baby. The darker meat of chicken legs contains twice as much iron and zinc as the lighter meat.

TOP TIP
Once babies are eating a varied diet, you may find that some foods, such as raisins, may appear in your baby's stools in their natural state. Don't worry; this is quite normal.

Chicken with sweetcorn and rice

2 chicken legs, skinned (about 250g/9oz in total)
1 bay leaf
sprig of parsley
3 black peppercorns
400ml (14fl oz) Chicken Stock (see page 124)
15g (½oz) unsalted butter
1 tbsp flour
40g (1½oz) tinned or frozen sweetcorn
75g (3oz) cooked basmati rice

Put the chicken in a saucepan together with the bay leaf, parsley and peppercorns and pour over the stock. Bring to the boil, then cover with a lid and simmer gently for 40 minutes or until the chicken is tender and cooked through.

Remove the chicken from the bone and chop into small pieces. Strain the stock and reserve. Melt the butter in a pan, stir in the flour and cook for 1 minute. Gradually whisk in the stock, bring to the boil and then cook for 1 minute. Stir in the sweetcorn and continue to cook for a couple of minutes. Mix together the chopped chicken, rice, stock and sweetcorn. Purée the mixture for younger babies.

Creamy chicken and vegetables

9–12 MONTHS

MAKES 3 PORTIONS

COOKING TIME: 17 MINS

SUITABLE FOR FREEZING

1 tbsp vegetable oil
40g (1½oz) chopped onion
2 medium carrots, peeled and chopped
75g (3oz) button mushrooms, wiped and sliced
1 tbsp flour
150ml (5fl oz) Chicken Stock (see page 124)
4 tbsp milk
50g (2oz) cooked chicken, chopped
25g (1oz) Cheddar cheese, grated

Using leftover roast chicken, this makes a nutritious and tasty dish for your baby. If you don't have any cooked chicken, poach half a chicken breast in some chicken stock for about 6 minutes or until cooked through.

Heat the oil in a saucepan and sauté the onion and carrots for 5 minutes, stirring occasionally. Add the mushrooms and sauté for 3 minutes. Stir in the flour and continue to cook for 1 minute. Gradually stir in the stock and the milk. Bring to the boil, then lower the heat and cook for 5 minutes. Stir in the chicken and cook for 1 more minute. Remove from the heat and stir in the cheese until melted. Either chop into small pieces or purée for your baby.

This tasty recipe will help encourage your baby to enjoy eating red meat.

My first spaghetti Bolognese

1½ tbsp vegetable oil
1 clove garlic, peeled and crushed
40g (1½oz) chopped onion
1 medium carrot, peeled and grated
75g (3oz) button mushrooms, wiped and sliced
150g (5oz) lean minced beef
125ml (4fl oz) passata
200ml (7fl oz) Chicken Stock (see page 124)
few drops of Worcestershire sauce
pinch of brown sugar
1 bay leaf
50g (2oz) spaghetti

Heat 1 tbsp oil in a saucepan and sauté the garlic and onion for 2 minutes. Add the grated carrot and sauté for 2 minutes more. Pour in the remaining oil and sauté the mushrooms for about 3 minutes.

Meanwhile, sauté the minced beef in a dry frying pan until browned and then add to the vegetables together with the passata, stock, Worcestershire sauce, sugar and bay leaf. Cover the saucepan with a lid and simmer for about 15 minutes. Cook the spaghetti according to the packet instructions, but without adding any salt.

Purée the cooked meat using a hand-held electric blender for a smoother texture. Chop up the spaghetti into short lengths and stir into the Bolognese sauce.

Old-fashioned beef casserole

The onions and carrots in this recipe give the beef a wonderful flavour and the long slow cooking makes it beautifully tender.

TOP TIP
If your baby doesn't like eating meat, you need to ensure that she's getting enough iron, so include foods in her diet like lentils, dark green leafy vegetables and fortified breakfast cereals.

1 onion, peeled and sliced
1½ tbsp vegetable oil
225g (8oz) lean stewing (blade or round) steak, cut into chunks
2 carrots, peeled and sliced
300g (11oz) potatoes, peeled and diced
1 tbsp chopped fresh parsley
450ml (16fl oz) Chicken Stock (see page 124)

Pre-heat the oven to 150°C/300°F/Gas 2. Sauté the onion in the vegetable oil in a flame-proof casserole until lightly golden. Add the beef and sauté until browned. Tip in the carrots, potatoes and parsley, pour over the stock and bring the mixture to the boil. Cover with a lid, transfer the casserole to the pre-heated oven and cook until for about 2 hours until the meat is really tender (adding extra stock if necessary). Chop into small pieces or, for younger babies, blend to a purée of the desired consistency.

Tender casserole of lamb

9–12 MONTHS

MAKES 4 PORTIONS

COOKING TIME: 1 HOUR

SUITABLE FOR FREEZING

2 lamb cutlets (about 160g/5½oz in total)
½ small onion, peeled and chopped
200g (7oz) potatoes, peeled and diced
110g (4oz) carrots, peeled and sliced
2 tomatoes, skinned, deseeded and chopped
(see page 126)
125ml (4fl oz) Chicken Stock (see page 124)

Pre-heat the oven to 180°C/350°F/Gas 4. Put the lamb cutlets, vegetables and stock into a small casserole, cover with a lid and cook in the pre-heated oven for about 1 hour until the lamb is tender. Chop into small pieces, or purée for younger babies.

Cooking lamb in a casserole with vegetables and stock makes it sufficiently tender and moist for your baby.

TOP TIP
Once your baby starts feeding herself, you may find that mealtimes take a lot longer, so try to allow for this.

9–12 MONTHS

MAKES 6 PORTIONS

COOKING TIME: 30–35 MINS

SUITABLE FOR FREEZING

This is a quicker version of making rice pudding, cooking it on top of the stove rather than in the oven.

TOP TIP
After the age of one year, if your child is fussy and eats only a small variety of foods, continuing with a standard infant formula milk or follow-on milk instead of using cow's milk might be beneficial.

Quick rice pudding

50g (2oz) pudding rice
600ml (1 pint) milk
1–2 tbsp caster sugar
1 vanilla pod or ½ tsp vanilla essence

Put the rice, milk and sugar in a heavy-bottomed saucepan. Split the vanilla pod, if using, and scrape the seeds into the pan, or add the vanilla essence. Bring to the boil, then reduce the heat, cover with a lid and simmer for 30–35 minutes, stirring occasionally. Mix with fruit or one of the toppings below.

- dried apricot purée
- stewed apple and pear
- fruit compote (Bon Maman fruit compote is good)
- low-sugar strawberry jam
- a little maple syrup
- strawberry purée – cook some strawberries, strain away some of the liquid, then purée, pass through a sieve and stir in a little icing sugar to taste

9–12 MONTHS

MAKES 2 PORTIONS

COOKING TIME: 7–8 MINS

SUITABLE FOR FREEZING

This dish is good on its own, or you could mix the fruit with yoghurt or stir into rice pudding.

Nectarine and strawberry with vanilla

2 nectarines or peaches, skinned and chopped (see page 125)
75g (3oz) strawberries, hulled and quartered
1 vanilla pod

Put the nectarines and strawberries into a heavy-bottomed saucepan. Split the vanilla pod and, using a sharp knife, scrape out the seeds and add to the fruit together with the pod. Cover with a lid and cook over a gentle heat for 7–8 minutes. Remove the vanilla pod and mash or chop the fruit.

9–12 MONTHS

MAKES 1 PORTION

COOKING TIME: 2 MINS

UNSUITABLE FOR FREEZING

Bananas are easy to digest and provide a good source of energy for your baby.

Yummy banana

15g (½oz) unsalted butter
1 small banana, peeled and sliced
3 tbsp freshly squeezed orange juice

Melt the butter in a small frying pan or saucepan and sauté the banana for 1 minute. Pour over the orange juice and cook for another minute. Mash with a fork.

9–12 MONTHS

 MAKES 2 PORTIONS

 COOKING TIME: NONE

❄ UNSUITABLE FOR FREEZING

This dish makes a great way to start the day. Serve it as it is or mix with some yoghurt.

TOP TIP
Never leave your baby alone while she is eating. Sometimes babies try to swallow food without chewing it and choking can be a real hazard. If your baby chokes, do not try to fish the food from the back of her mouth as you may only end up pushing it further down her throat. Tip her face down over your lap with her head lower than her stomach and slap her firmly between the shoulder blades to dislodge the food. If the food is coughed up into her mouth, then carefully remove it.

Fruity muesli

50g (2oz) rolled oats
15g (½oz) wheatgerm
25g (1oz) ready-to-eat dried apricots, chopped
150ml (5fl oz) freshly squeezed orange juice
1 apple, peeled and grated

Mix the oats together with the wheatgerm and apricots. Pour over the orange juice and leave to soak for at least 5 minutes. Stir in the grated apple and blitz for a few seconds using a hand-held electric blender.

Basics

Vegetable stock

1 onion, peeled
1 clove garlic, peeled
2 large carrots, peeled
1 large leek, washed
1 stick celery, trimmed
1 tbsp olive oil
850ml (29fl oz) cold water
1 bouquet garni or a mixture of fresh herbs
(e.g. sprig of thyme, parsley, oregano and a bay leaf)
4 black peppercorns

Roughly chop all the vegetables. Heat the oil in a large, heavy-bottomed saucepan and sauté the onion and garlic for 2 minutes. Add the rest of the vegetables and sweat in the oil without browning for 5 minutes, covering with a lid if you like.

Pour in the water and bring to the boil, then add the bouquet garni and peppercorns. Reduce the heat, cover with the lid and simmer for 1 hour.

Leave to cool for about 2 hours, then strain through a sieve. Squeeze the remaining juices out of the vegetables by pushing them down in the sieve with a potato masher.

6 MONTHS +

MAKES 600ML (1 PINT)

COOKING TIME:
1 HOUR 7 MINS

SUITABLE FOR FREEZING
BUT NOT SUITABLE FOR
RE-FREEZING IN A PURÉE

It is best to use homemade stock when cooking for a young baby as stock cubes are high in salt and therefore unsuitable for babies under a year. In addition, it is important to use fresh and not previously frozen stock when making up baby purées that you intend to freeze. Vegetable stock is very easy to make and will keep in the fridge for up to a week.

6 MONTHS +

MAKES 1.8 LITRES (3 PINTS)

COOKING TIME: 1½ HOURS

SUITABLE FOR FREEZING BUT
NOT SUITABLE FOR RE-FREEZING
IN A PURÉE

Making your own chicken stock sounds laborious but it is actually very easy. Simply take the carcass from a roast chicken to form the basis of your stock or use some chicken bones. The stock will keep in the fridge for 3 days.

Chicken stock

carcass from a roast chicken or about 900g (2lb)
chicken bones, chopped into pieces
3 carrots, peeled
1 parsnip, peeled
1 leek, washed
2 onions, peeled
1 stick celery, trimmed
small bunch of parsley
1 sprig thyme
1 bay leaf
4 black peppercorns
2 litres (3½ pints) boiling water

Put the carcass into a large, heavy-based saucepan. Roughly chop all the vegetables and add to the pan together with the herbs and peppercorns. Pour over the water, bring to the boil and then remove all the surface sediment with a slotted spoon. Half cover the pan and simmer gently for 1½ hours or until the liquid is reduced by half.

Allow to cool, then leave in the fridge overnight. Remove any congealed fat from the top in the morning. Strain the chicken and vegetables to make the stock.

Basic cheese sauce

15g (½oz) unsalted butter
15g (½oz) plain flour
150ml (5fl oz) milk
30g (1oz) Gruyère cheese, grated
2 tbsp Parmesan cheese, grated
2 tbsp mascarpone

Melt the butter in a saucepan, stir in the flour to
make a smooth paste and cook for 1 minute. Gradually
stir in the milk, bring to the boil and cook for a few
minutes over a low heat until thickened and smooth.
Take off the heat, stir in the Gruyère and Parmesan
until melted, then stir in the mascarpone.

 MAKES 3 PORTIONS

 SUITABLE FOR FREEZING

You can make this in
batches and freeze it. It
blends well with cooked
vegetables, fish or it is also
delicious served as a sauce
with tiny pasta shapes.

Skinning tomatoes and peaches/nectarines

Plunge the tomatoes in boiling water for 30 seconds.
Transfer to cold water, then skin, deseed and chop.
For peaches/nectarines, score a cross on the base
of each fruit, then submerge in boiling water for
1 minute. Skin, cut in half, discarding the stone,
and chop the flesh.

Index

Page numbers in **bold** indicate a recipe where the entry is a main ingredient.

Author's Acknowledgements

I would like to thank the following for their help on this book: Sarah Lavelle, Dave King, Kate Parker, Caroline King, Dr Jane Morgan, Dr Mary Fewtrell, Dagmar Vesely, Jo Harris, Carey Smith, Katherine Hockley, and all at Smith & Gilmour. Thanks also to the mothers and babies who feature in the book: Claire and Leo Bowers, Lauren and Aaron Breslauer, Helena and Tomas Caldon, Beverley and Chase Calvert, Laura and Charlie Davies, Rosie and Maia Hallam, Daniella and Luca Pillitto, and Julie and Emily Zimmerman.

About the Author

Annabel Karmel is a leading author on cooking for children and has written 14 bestselling books that are sold all over the world. After the tragic loss of her first child, who died of a rare viral disease aged just three months, Annabel wrote her first book, *The Complete Baby and Toddler Meal Planner*, now an international bestseller. A mother of three, she is an expert in devising tasty and nutritious meals for children without the need for parents to spend hours in the kitchen. Annabel was awarded an MBE for services to child nutrition in 2006. Annabel writes regularly for national newspapers and magazines and appears frequently on radio and television as the UK's top expert on children's nutritional issues. To buy other titles by Annabel Karmel, visit www.randomhouse.co.uk or Annabel's own website, www.annabelkarmel.com.

Annabel Karmel's

make your own...

I recognise that how you feed your baby is one of the most important decisions you make for your child, so I have devised a new range of equipment and food to help you. The range provides everything you need to make fresh food for your baby or toddler. It includes:

- **Baby Food Grinder**
- **Electric Hand Blender**
- **Food Cube Trays**
- **Rocket Ice Lolly Moulds**
- **Sauces and Pastas**

All are available from **Boots** stores and from **www.Boots.com**. For delicious recipes from the range, visit my website **www.annabelkarmel.com**

It's good to be a bit fussy about what you eat these days. That's why I have created a new range of tasty, yet healthy meals made especially for children. They're balanced, mouth-watering meals for young children without the fuss. What's more, I'm very fussy about what goes into them so I only use the best natural ingredients.

- **Scrummy Chicken Dumplings with Rice**
- **Mummy's Favorite Salmon and Cod Fish Pie**
- **Beef Cottage Pie**
- **Yummy Chicken Curry**
- **Hidden Vegetable Pasta**
- **Cheeky Chicken and Potato Pie**
- **Teddy Bear Pizzas**

Look for **Eat Fussy** in the chilled section of your local supermarket: just ask!